Eureka Ill
Oct, 8 - 1910

Thumb vital
fore finger. point out. To a mouse Bross
3 + 4 finger; excitment

Everett Rinker
Fable Grove.
Ill.

Jan. 18, 1911

Get the feeling in what
you say. See what you
are talking about

PUBLIC SPEAKING

A Treatise on Delivery

WITH SELECTIONS FOR DECLAIMING

BY

EDWIN DUBOIS SHURTER

ASSOCIATE PROFESSOR OF ORATORY IN THE
UNIVERSITY OF TEXAS

ALLYN AND BACON
Boston and Chicago

Norwood Press
J. S. Cushing & Co. — Berwick & Smith Co.
Norwood, Mass., U.S.A.

PREFACE.

THIS book is intended to help those who would speak well in public. It deals not so much with What to Say as How To Say It; and is designed to prepare students for subsequent training in formal oratory, debate, and extempore speaking.

Most of the books that deal with the art of delivery belong to one of two general classes: (1) those containing generalizations that are all very good, but of no practical utility to the student of speaking; (2) those that are full of elocutionary directions and rules, that lean toward dramatic reading rather than public speaking, and stress mechanics rather than mentality. The treatment in this volume aims to be more specific than the one and less technical than the other. The mental requirements for speaking are emphasized throughout. Experience has shown that students should, at the outset, be put on thought-analysis, as is outlined in Chapter I; that the idea of *thought*-expression should be firmly fixed before the consideration of technique.

Since public speaking is largely an art, no book of this nature can wholly supply a method or supplant a teacher. A few rules are given in the text, but these are rather principles to be grasped than rules to be memorized; and even then, perhaps, the able teacher can often make an example more effective without any rule.

The author gratefully acknowledges his indebtedness to Professor Brainard G. Smith, for the use made of his

Reading and Speaking; to Messrs. Lee and Shepard, for permission to adapt, in Chapter I of this volume, portions of Kirby's exposition on "The Mental Content of Language," Part II, Chapter I, of his *Public Speaking and Reading,* and also for permission to use the selections from Phillips's orations and lectures; to Professor Hiram Corson, for permission to quote from his *The Voice and Spiritual Education;* to Harper and Brothers, for the selections from Curtis's *Orations and Addresses;* to Funk and Wagnalls Co., for the extracts from Sheppard's *Before an Audience;* to Longmans, Green and Co., for the quotations from Higginson's *Hints on Writing and Speech-making;* to Houghton, Mifflin and Co., for the quotations from Emerson's *Essays;* to Mr. Elbert Hubbard, for the selections from his writings; to The Gammel Book Co., of Austin, Texas, for permission to reprint several selections from the author's *The Modern American Speaker.*

If this book shall stimulate the young speaker to work, or make the method of working plainer and easier, or shall help dispel from his mind any erroneous and fanciful notions often associated with the art of public speaking, the author's object will be fulfilled.

E. D. S.

THE UNIVERSITY OF TEXAS,
September, 1903.

CONTENTS.

INTRODUCTION.

IN his little book on *Hints on Writing and Speech-making*, Colonel Thomas Wentworth Higginson points out that "the number of graduates going forth each year from our American colleges must be several thousand, since the number of undergraduates is more than twenty thousand. If we add those who are graduates of academies . . . the figures will be greatly swelled. The majority of all these graduates will be called upon, at some time or other during their lives, to make a speech, as will also thousands of young Americans who have never seen the inside of college or academy." Speech-making, as Colonel Higginson suggests, is a condition of American life and government. True, newspapers and magazines have in some ways affected the requirements for the public speaker, but they have by no means supplanted him, and they never will. The proof of this assertion lies not alone in the peculiar social and political demands under a republican form of government, but is inherent in human nature itself. If men are moved by the printed word, must they not be aroused still more by the spoken word? If the author can convince through the lifeless type, how much more effectively can men's sensibilities be touched through the directness and earnestness of the living man! "In these days," says Ex-Premier Salisbury, "whether we like it or not, power is with the tongue, power is with those who can speak." And Gladstone declared, "All time and money spent in training the voice and the body is an investment that pays a larger interest than any other."

1

The school and college graduates referred to by Colonel Higginson will become — or should become — leaders in moulding and directing public opinion in their respective communities. Now, if education should help prepare our school and college graduates for the duties and privileges of citizenship — and who will say that it should not? — the question arises, Are our schools and colleges performing their duty in the training of public speakers? In some institutions, yes; in many others, no. There has been, even during the past ten years, a marked improvement in this regard, but yet there is no generally accepted opinion that instruction in public speaking demands a place in school and college curriculum.

Why this seeming indifference? In part, at least, because of a widespread prejudice among educators against so-called " elocutionary " training. It must be admitted that the prejudice is well founded. " Long-haired men and short-haired women," with what Emerson calls a " patty-pan ebullition," have gone about the country giving " readings " wherein self-conscious posing, and the artificial vocalizing of hothouse " literature," have long afflicted a patient public. Now, the association of this brand with the idea of public speaking is most unfortunate. I am not pooh-poohing all public readings, by any means. The intelligent and sympathetic oral interpretation of good literature is certainly an enviable accomplishment, and of great educational value; but even that is not public speaking. Much less so, the dramatic " reading " above described. But, granting this distinction, the objector interposes, " Speaking cannot be taught." And in this connection I wish briefly to notice some of the fallacies relative to instruction along these lines : —

1. *" Training makes one self-conscious and artificial."* This may at times be true, but it all depends upon the quality and quantity of the training. The exemplification of this

objection is seen in the crude attempts of persons who have mastered the beginnings of an art, and mistaken them for the end. Certainly the masters of the art of speech, both ancient and modern, did not become masters without laborious and long-continued training. Such training was the lifelong work of the Greek and Roman orators. Curran, the celebrated Irish orator, was so handicapped in his youth that he was called "stuttering Jack Curran." He said of himself, "My friends despaired of my ever making a speaker, but I would not give it up." Says one of his friends, "He turned his shrill and stumbling brogue into a flexible, sustained, and finely modulated voice; his action became free and forcible; and he acquired perfect readiness in thinking on his legs." With reference to both matter and manner, Webster said of himself: "When I was a young man, and for several years after I had acquired a respectable degree of eminence in my profession, my style was bombastic in the extreme. Some kind friend was good enough to point out that fact to me, and I determined to correct it, if labor could do it. Whether it has been corrected or not, no small part of my life has been spent in the attempt."

2. "*The orator is born, not made.*" True, in a sense, but we must qualify and distinguish. No man will ever be a great orator without certain inborn qualities and the oratorical instinct. But it does not follow that a young man cannot be taught to correct bad habits of speech and form better habits; to train himself, during his school or college course, in speaking before an audience; to conquer stage-fright, and develop self-control, ease, and power. He may not have in him the making of an orator; but he can, by due attention and systematic work, acquire such knowledge and skill as to increase his effectiveness as a public speaker. And if he has that indefinable quality termed the "oratorical instinct,"

training is none the less necessary to make him an orator No orator is born any more than an artist or a musician is born. The orator who relies solely on his birth is never heard from.

3. "*Be in earnest; forget about yourself and think only of your subject.*" This is most excellent advice. In the actual process of speech-making, the less one thinks about himself, and the more intensely he thinks about his subject, the more effective his delivery. "Clearness, force, and earnestness are the qualities which produce conviction." But we must distinguish between the end and the means to such end. In the period of preliminary training, perhaps the last thing the young speaker should do is to forget about himself. He may be dead in earnest about his subject, but such earnestness is ineffective as to his audience unless he speaks, for instance, so that he can be heard. He may have a hundred and one mannerisms, vocal and physical, that most seriously intervene between his earnestness and those to whom he would convey his thought. Says Cicero, in his *De Oratore*, "What Socrates used to say, that 'all men are sufficiently eloquent in that which they understand,' is very plausible, but not true. It would have been nearer the truth to say that no man can be eloquent on a subject that he does not understand; and that, if he understands a subject never so well, but is ignorant of how to form and polish his speech, he cannot express himself eloquently even about what he does understand."

4. "*Be natural, and you will speak well.*" This, too, is a most excellent direction, so far as it applies to the avoidance of artificial and mechanical methods in the act of speaking; but what do we mean by being "natural"? Talking through the nose or teeth, or in the throat, or at the walls, may seem natural to many; but these are matters of habit rather than of nature. Students who in their school or college course first give attention to the manner of their speech, bring to the

study certain habits. These habits may be good or bad. The good habits need developing and strengthening; the bad represent sundry faults, some curable, many needing to be eradicated and supplanted, all capable of improvement. Now, these bad habits are not natural, in the sense that they are true exponents of nature. They are, rather, a cultivated unnaturalness. We must therefore be careful not to confound habit with nature, peculiarity with individuality. On this "being natural" fallacy, Professor Hiram Corson, in his little book, *The Voice and Spiritual Education,* says: "'Enter into the *spirit* of what you read, read *naturally,* and you will read well,' is about the sum and substance of what Archbishop Whately teaches on the subject, in his *Elements of Rhetoric.* Similar advice might with equal propriety be given to a clumsy, stiff-jointed clodhopper in regard to dancing, 'Enter into the spirit of the dance, dance naturally, and you will dance well.' The more he might enter into the spirit of the dance, the more he might emphasize his stiff-jointedness and clodhopperishness."

There is this further phase of the problem: in addition to natural or normal faults of speech, the presence of an audience often superimposes abnormal ones. If one, without training or practice, could rise and face an audience, large or small, and speak with the interest, vivacity, earnestness, and naturalness that he would employ in good conversation, there would be no need of this book or of teachers of expression. But the most casual observation shows that this is not the case.

To learn to speak, then, one must in some way (1) acquire the right mental attitude toward his message and his audience; and (2), as a means to this end, remove, so far as possible, vocal and bodily limitations that hinder the most effective delivery of the thought. There are some who assert that if the first requirement be attained, the second will naturally and necessarily follow. This position doubtless represents the reaction from the mechanical, artificial, "elocutionary" methods, but like most reactions, the truth probably lies midway. It is better, of course, to have mind-action and a rough mechanism, than a finished method and no motive power; but it does not follow that some attention should not be paid to the voice and body as agents of expression.

In short, public speaking is an art, and it does not come by chance. To acquire this art requires work — conscientious, systematic, continuous preparation and practice. Like every other study, we get out of it what we put in. Any young person who expects to speak in public should, at the outset, disabuse his mind of the idea that a term's or a year's lessons in oratory will turn him out a finished product. Years of study and practice are required, and then no one can be said to have acquired perfection in the art. We listen to an effective speaker, and remark how easily his periods roll out. But we forget that behind them lies a long course of study and self-discipline, study not necessarily of any particular system of expression, nor under any teacher, but certainly not without training in the school of experience. Fortunate that young speaker whose first efforts are directed along right lines, and whose first experiences are had under helpful conditions.

CHAPTER I.

THE NATURE AND BASIS OF PUBLIC SPEAKING.

Public Speaking Defined. — What is public speaking? It is speaking to a collection of individuals. Its purposes are to convey thought, to mould opinion, and to awaken feeling. Any one or all of these purposes may be present in a given address, but in any case there is thought to be conveyed, whether in the form of exposition, argument, or appeal. Public speaking, then, as the term is used in this book, is speaking in public with the purpose of convincing and persuading, and not for entertainment simply, which is usually the purpose in reciting, dramatic reading, or acting.

Tests of the Best Public Speaking. — You are to speak to ten, one hundred, or one thousand people collectively — your audience. How best speak to them for the purposes of instructing, convincing, or persuading? This question is best answered by asking, How best speak when you are talking to any one of them? That is, the criteria of the best public speaking are those of the best conversation, — not the most showy or noisy, but the *best*, from the standpoint of effectiveness. In the conveyance and lodgement of thought, what constitutes effectiveness in conversation? Among other things, a good conversationalist must possess the qualities of clearness, directness, simplicity, vivacity, spontaneity, and sincerity. Hence these same qualities must be effective in public speech.

What Public Speaking is Not. — Eliminate, at the outset, the extraneous or fanciful ideas often connected with the art of speaking in public. A pleasing, musical voice is an added charm, but not indispensable. Grace is desirable, but a fine carriage or pretty gestures do not carry a cause or win a verdict. Nor is there *any* ready-made prescription. Many students seek instruction in oratory who seem to imagine that the teacher can furnish them with some patent device whereby they will become proficient in the art. Banish from your mind any thought that this or that "system," this or that "method," will make you an orator, or even — what is far more to our purpose — an effective public speaker. No method but your own — the expression of your individuality — will ever make you any sort of a speaker other than a parrot or a machine. Be yourself, not a mere imitator. Certain principles are fundamental, but expression will be as varied as individualities. Avoid any "system" that would cast all speakers in the same mould. Aim not to become a Demosthenes or Cicero, a Webster or Clay, but aim for the best and most effective expression of Yourself. Above all, eschew any ambition to become "eloquent," as the term is commonly used, — "to soar among the constellations and strew the floor with star-dust." Furthermore, true eloquence never comes from a conscious effort toward that in itself. "It comes, if it come at all, like the outbreak of a fountain from the earth, or the bursting forth of volcanic fires, with spontaneous, original, native force." The speaker "should pray to be delivered from the ambition to be eloquent," says Dr. Lyman Abbott, "by an ambition to win a result; be careless of admiration and covetous of practical fruits in his auditors' lives. Without this moral preparation he will be a mere declaimer; with it he may be an effective speaker. And whether he is what men call an orator or not is a matter of no consequence."

The Basis of Public Speaking: Clear, Orderly, Intense Thinking. — Public speaking, then, being the communication of thought, it follows that you must have something to say; and a clear and vivid concept of this something to say must be present to the mind at the moment of its utterance. Public speaking is the science and art of thinking aloud. If there is any one thing that the modern audience wish to be delivered from, it is mere volubility, with thought in inverse proportion. The most inveterate bore in modern assemblies is the chronic talker — the man who has nothing to say and is forever saying it. So we can well understand Lowell's suggested addition to the Beatitudes, "Blessed is he who hath nothing to say — and cannot be persuaded to say it."

Processes in the Preparation of an Address for Delivery.

1. *The Selection of an Address.* — Oratorical composition is not within the province of this book; it is therefore assumed that you have something to say. With young speakers, who have as yet neither the material nor the ability for original composition, it is often quite as well to borrow another's thoughts and words, for the purposes of training in expression. Only selections worth memorizing should be chosen. Literature is full of such selections adaptable to speaking. The memorizing of choice selections from the best literature has been sadly neglected in our modern educational system. Its value successful public speakers have long recognized. It furnishes a storehouse of illustration and expression; it aids the memory, furnishes a means of culture, and is a never-failing source of pleasure. Further, in class-room work, it affords a common basis of study and reference for teacher and class.

2. *Perspective.* — You have an address to prepare for delivery. Let us note some of the steps in such preparation. If

the address be not original, the first step is to get a proper perspective of the thought as a whole; for just as in the preparation of an original address the audience and occasion must be carefully considered, so, in preparation for the delivery of another's thought, must the student go outside of the printed words and study the writer or speaker, and the circumstances surrounding the first writing or delivery. Truly to interpret and sympathetically to express another's words one must know the author, and live again in his experiences at the time he gave his thought to the world. Moreover, such external study is desirable, in order that the speaker may breathe the atmosphere of a particular address, — be put in the proper mood[1] for its delivery.

3. *The Theme of the Address.* — Turning now to the content of the address itself, the student must first note the gist of the discourse as a whole. What is the thought, in a nutshell? Grip it. The introductory, explanatory, and modifying ideas must be noted, and subordinated to the essential and controlling ideas. The controlling ideas will be found in those key-words or sentences that together express the theme of the discourse. This theme must be grasped, and must dominate the expression.

4. *Paragraphs.* — Every paragraph of the address, if well constructed, represents a unit in the development of the thought; and each paragraph, in turn, denotes a progressive transition in the thought movement. A paragraph will usually contain a key-sentence, around which the thought of that paragraph clusters. It is for the speaker to discover this key-sentence, make it stand out in the utterance, and subordinate the matter of less relative importance.

[1] " Less intensive degrees of emotion are called moods. It is a general rule that the duration of emotion varies inversely with its intensity; so that moods are more permanent states of mind than emotions proper." — SCRIPTURE: *Thinking, Feeling, Doing,* p. 227.

5. *Sentences.* — Sentences are made up of ideas and express complete thoughts. In every sentence the two leading ideas always are, first, something you are speaking of, and second, what you say of that something; or, subject and predicate. In addition to these two primary ideas, every sentence may have numerous words, phrases, and clauses that limit or qualify the thought. For the purposes of expression, the student should first discover these two leading ideas. Following the first sentence in any selection, he should note what new idea each sentence contains, and what ideas are merely repetitions or echoes of preceding sentences. He should note the words that bear the burden of this new idea, and in speaking, of course, express the new or important ideas as such to the hearers.

6. *Words.* — Thought is conveyed by means of words; but words as such are meaningless. They are simply signs of ideas. The mere utterance of words may be as expressionless as the vocalizing of an uneducated deaf-mute. For example, take the following word-combination which the man in one of George Eliot's novels found so much comfort in repeating: "Sihon, King of the Amorites, for his mercy endureth forever. And Og, King of Bashan, for his mercy endureth forever." Beware, then, of uttering words instead of thoughts.

Observing the foregoing suggestions, study the following selections : —

CONSERVATISM.

Speaking of conservatism, George William Curtis said : —
"A friend of mine was a student of Couture the painter, in Paris. One day the master came and looked over the pupil's drawing and said to him, 'My friend, that line should go so'; and indicated it lightly on the paper with his pencil. To prove the accuracy of the master's eye, the

pupil rubbed out the correction and left the line.   The next day Couture came, and looking over the drawing, stopped in surprise.   'That's curious,' said he, 'I thought I altered that.   This line goes so,' he added, and drew it firmly in black upon the paper.   Again the pupil rubbed out the correction.   The next day the master came again, stopped short when he saw the drawing, looked at it a moment without speaking; then, with his thumb-nail, he cut quite through the paper.   'That's the way this line ought to go,' he said, and passed on.

"So the hearts and minds of our fathers marked the line of our true development.   Conservatism rubbed it out.   The Missouri struggle emphasized the line again.   Conservatism rubbed it out.   The tragedy of Kansas drew the line more sternly.   Conservatism rubbed it out.   Then, at last, the Divine finger drew in fire and blood, sharply, sharply, through our wailing homes, through our torn and bleeding country, through our very quivering hearts, the line of liberty, and justice, and equal rights; and conservatism might as well try to rub out the rainbow from the heavens, as to erase this, the decision of the age."

THE HOME AND THE REPUBLIC.

In an address delivered at Elberton, Georgia, in June, 1889, Henry W. Grady said : —

"I went to Washington the other day, and as I stood on Capitol Hill my heart beat quick as I looked at the towering marble of my country's Capitol, and the mist gathered in my eyes as I thought of its tremendous significance, — the army, and the Treasury, and the courts, and Congress, and the President, and all that was gathered there.   And I felt that the sun in all its course could not look down upon a better sight than that majestic home of the Republic that had taught the world its best lessons in liberty.

"Two days afterwards I went to visit a friend in the country, — a modest man, with a quiet country home. It was just a simple, unpretentious house, set about with great big trees, encircled in meadow and fields rich with the promise of harvest. The fragrance of pink and hollyhock in the front yard was mingled with the aroma of the orchard and of the garden, and resonant with the cluck of poultry and the hum of bees. Inside was quiet, cleanliness, thrift, and comfort. Outside there stood my friend — master of his land and master of himself. There was his old father, an aged, trembling man, happy in the heart and home of his son. And as they started to their home the hands of the old man went down on the young man's shoulders, laying there the unspeakable blessing of an honored and grateful father, and ennobling it with the knighthood of the Fifth Commandment. . . . And I saw the night come down on that home, falling gently as from the wings of an unseen dove, and the old man, while a startled bird called from the forest, and the trees shrilled with the cricket's cry, and the stars were swarming in the sky, got the family around him, and taking the old Bible from the table, called them to their knees, while he closed the record of that simple day by calling down God's blessing on that family and that home.

"And while I gazed, the vision of the marble Capitol faded. Forgotten were its treasures and its majesty, and I said, 'O, surely, here in the hearts of the people at last are lodged the strength and responsibilities of this government, the hope and promise of this Republic.'"

In any selection for delivery, preliminary study, with a view of comprehending and assimilating the thought and feeling, should always precede any attempt to speak. After such study, speak colloquially — as you would in conversation — making your delivery thoughtful, earnest, direct, strong *talk.*

The general suggestions previously made in this chapter are summarized and made more specific in the appended directions and questions. It will be found profitable to write out a report of your selection, answering fully all the following whenever an answer is possible.

The Mastery of an Address: Questions and Suggestions.

1. Who is the author or speaker? Under what circumstances was the selection first written or spoken? If possible, read the article or address in full.

2. Read the selection silently, and re-read until you grasp its meaning as a whole. Express in a single sentence the gist of the whole selection.

3. Can you see the thought-movement from beginning to end? Is the line of thought logical and consecutive? Do the paragraphs mark the natural divisions? If not, re-paragraph; then state, in a single sentence, the central thought of each paragraph.

4. What is the first new idea in each sentence? (Underscore once.) What word, phrase, or clause in each sentence carries the principal idea? (Underscore twice.) Note that the answers to these two questions may sometimes be identical.

5. What word or group of words in each sentence expresses a single idea? Separate these groups by vertical lines.

6. Dwell on the meaning of each word. Note the relative importance of each word as expressive of the thought. Do you know the meaning of every proper name? Comment on words of peculiar significance.

7. Analyze the language in order to call up the associated ideas. What associated ideas present themselves to your mind?

8. Explain all historical or other allusions.

9. Analyze the selection to find its emotion. Note the varied and changing emotions. What is the predominant emotion or atmosphere of the selection? Think over the selection, and wait until the emotion matures.

10. In the process of memorizing, observe the following steps: (1) Link the ideas together in a chain of thought. Close the eyes and follow the thought of the speech through without vocalizing a word. (2) With closed eyes try to express orally the chain of ideas in the words of the writer. Wherever difficulty arises, study that particular part. Do not memorize the words by a parrot-like repetition. It is not necessary to use in minutest detail the exact words of the author. (3) Now talk the address to yourself or to an imaginary hearer, as you would converse. Do not try to " speak " or gesticulate until the speech is a part of yourself. Make the thought your thought, the words your words. Re-create the thoughts and emotions of the speech, — you are then prepared to use your mind and feelings in speaking it to your audience.

This preliminary preparation is not the easiest process, but it outlines the only proper method of approaching the delivery of any address. Clear expression is born of clear thought. Unless thought and emotion are present in the act of delivery, there can be no effective speaking. Public speaking, we might say, is the oral reproduction of one's own or another's ideas, — in either case, of ideas previously thought out, classified, and assimilated. When thought, not the vocalizing of words merely, becomes the primary object, public speaking is an incomparable means for mental training. Consider the sustained mental effort, in the midst of distractions such as other experiences rarely involve, that is required in a successful public address. The student in his room may alternately think and muse. The public speaker *must* think, intensely, clearly, consecutively, moving by natural transitions from idea to idea; for any musing or wool-gathering in the presence of an audience is fatal.

We thus see that there must be a mental and emotional basis for public speaking. But this alone is not enough. Thought must be communicated through a physical medium. This medium is the voice and the body. It is therefore necessary to give some attention to the technique of expression. This is set forth in succeeding chapters. It should be constantly borne in mind, however, that technique — the art side of our subject — is a means, not an end; and further, this end — the conveyance and impress of thought — must be constantly in mind, else there can be no true mastery of the means.

SUMMARY.

The best public speaking is enlarged and heightened conversation. The basis of effective speaking is clear and orderly thought, attained by a thorough analysis and assimilation of the discourse. Such thought-preparation must always precede, and thinking must always accompany, all efforts in the art of delivery.

CHAPTER II.

THE VOICE.

The Importance and the Possibility of Voice Culture. —
There are two means of expression, — by the voice and by the
body. For our purposes, the voice demands the first and
foremost attention. A clear, resonant, musical voice is
surely an enviable possession. "A good voice has a charm
in speech, as in song; oftentimes of itself enchains attention." In an article in *Scribner's Magazine* for June, 1901,
Senator Hoar says: "When every other faculty of the
orator is acquired, it sometimes almost seems as if voice
were nine-tenths, and everything else but one-tenth, of the
consummate orator. It is impossible to overrate the importance to his purpose of that matchless instrument, the
human voice."

This chief medium of expression, capable of conveying all
shades of thought with exquisite delicacy, be it in conversation, reading aloud, or public speech, the great instrument whereby the hearts of an audience may be made to
beat in unison, — is it not a matter for wonderment that we
do not give more attention to the training of the speaking
voice? What sort of a voice have you? High-pitched or
low? Throaty, hollow, or breathy? Have you ever asked
yourself, or had a good judge tell you? If you have a weak
or harsh, disagreeable voice, can anything be done to help
it? Certainly there can. We have gymnastics to straighten
the back, to develop the chest or any specially weak organ

17

or muscle. So are there gymnastics that will strengthen and improve the voice; but just as in all gymnastics, there must be systematic and continued practice before results will follow. A good voice is not altogether a freak of nature. We certainly do not act on this principle in dealing with the singing voice. While a "naturally" good voice is a boon, it is generally recognized that to be a really successful singer, one must take at least two or three years of special training. The same is true of the speaking voice, and the same training will produce equally satisfactory results. The trouble is, few speakers realize this, or have the patience and perseverance to undergo a training similar to that which we know is indispensable for the singer. The singer develops not only strength and volume of tone, but also improves the quality, or *timbre.* The same may be done by properly training the voice for speaking. If, then, the voice can be strengthened and controlled for speaking in public, it becomes apparent that this strengthening and controlling process should be gone through with in the preliminary stages of the development of the speaker. How many public speakers there are whose voices grate and grind on the nerves of the hearers, — voices whose defects a minimum of preliminary attention would at least have mended, if not wholly cured.

In the vocal and other exercises that are suggested in this and succeeding chapters, the question is perforce brought home to the mind of the student, What am I doing with my voice and body? Am I making the best use of them as mediums of expression? In other words, good habits are to be strengthened and perfected, bad habits are to be eliminated and better habits formed in their stead. To form a new habit in the place of an old one, we must give conscious attention, first, to the fault; and secondly, to the formation of the new habit. This, you say, makes you self-conscious.   True, but only *as a means to an end*.   Self-consciousness on the part of many public speakers to whom we are compelled to listen would be a blessed relief to the audience.   By this is meant, of course, consciousness of glaring faults for the purpose of correction.   The young speaker should first know what he is doing with his voice and his body.   After conscious attention to faults, *practice* — conscientious, systematic, continued practice, and then — practice again.   Cicero long ago taught that "the exertion and exercise of the voice, of the breath, of the whole body, and of the tongue itself, do not so much require art as labour."   Like every other art, if public speaking is one one-hundredth theory, it is ninety-nine one-hundredths practice.   The formation of this new habit to supplant the old is hard at first.   You have years of wrong practice to overcome; but by constant watchfulness and persistency the new habit becomes easier and easier until what was at first conscious, painful effort has become an accustomed practice, — a new habit.   In other words, the task is, through conscious attention for a time, to form other and better habits, which when firmly fixed will be as unconscious as were formerly the faulty ones.

How Speech is Effected. — It is unnecessary to treat in any detail the anatomy or physiology of the vocal organs.   We all know the process of voice-production, — how the column of air coming from the lungs through the trachea is arrested in the larynx by the vocal cords, which, vibrating, produce sound.   This sound, by various positions of the throat and mouth cavity, is converted into vowels, and by sundry interruptions and modifications through the action of the palate, tongue, teeth, and lips, the consonants are formed.   The various combinations of these vowel and consonant sounds constitute our spoken language.

Breathing. — Scientists tell us that man's vitality is measured by his lung capacity. The speaker needs vitality if he is to vitalize his audience. He needs the all-round, healthful physical training now generally recognized as essential to real education, and which Herbert Spencer calls "physical morality." And just as the athlete needs special training for a special event, so the speaker needs special gymnastics for the use of the breath. Breath is the stuff of which voice is made. To produce tone we must have breath coming from the lungs; to produce a strong tone, we must have breath in sufficient volume and force; to produce a sustained tone, we must have a generous supply of air stored in the lungs. Again, in ordinary breathing we inhale and exhale regularly — a constant stream of air going to and coming from the lungs. In speaking, however, we must inhale quickly at the pauses in our speech, and exhale slowly, converting the exhalations into vocal sounds. Now, we must learn to perform properly this inhaling and exhaling process. How often do we hear speakers gasp for breath at the beginning of a sentence, and perhaps audibly breathe out a generous supply at the end of a sentence. Or they inhale with a loud gasp on beginning, as though they had just come above the surface of the water, — swallow the sentence, as it were, — then bang out the first few words to "split the rafters," and soon subside to end the sentence in another gasp. They "get out of breath" and run down at the end of a sentence, like a clock that needs winding. This suggests the need not only of breath-quantity, but of breath-control.

And first, as to quantity. We know the different ways in which the chest capacity is enlarged whereby the lungs are filled with air. We may lift the shoulders and collar-bone and so enlarge the upper part of the chest. This is called clavicular or collar-bone breathing. This method is sometimes necessitated temporarily by disease, permanently by tight lacing, and is as bad for the voice as it is for the health. To use only the upper and smaller part of the conical shaped chest requires frequent respiration. By this method we secure the smallest supply of breath at the greatest expense of strength. Further, this method necessitates an attempt to control the breath in the throat, which was never intended for this purpose. It tends to cause the breath to come in spurts, or more air to escape than can be vocalized, making the voice trembling, jerky, wheezing, or "throaty." It causes a constrained position of the vocal organs, — a condition that is responsible for "clergyman's sore throat."

A second method of enlarging the chest is by extending the lower or floating ribs sideways. This is called costal or rib breathing. It has many advantages over the first method. It fills the middle portion of the lungs, and should be employed in connection with the third method, whereby the lower part of the lungs are reached. This is called abdominal, diaphragmatic, or deep breathing. The diaphragm contracts, moves downward, while at the same time the abdominal muscles expand the lower chest laterally, thus creating a large cavity for the air to enter. Now, the muscles that control respiration are partly voluntary and partly involuntary. By conscious attention we can learn to use them properly. Do you use the lower part of your lungs in respiration? If not, you must learn to do so. This is an exercise not for the voice only; athletes, and others who need their full lung capacity, acquire the habit of deep breathing. In forming this habit, give your primary attention to using the diaphragm, and the rib breathing will take care of itself; think of filling the lower part of the lungs. Place the hands above the hips, press firmly as you inhale, and you can soon learn if you are using the diaphragm in breathing. If not, use it, and practise using until it becomes an unconscious habit. Watch yourself when walking or reclining. The speaker cannot have a strong, pure, resonant, sustained tone unless he breathes deeply. This method gives him a reserve supply of air in the lungs. Further, the speaker frequently needs to control the voice with the diaphragm. This is the case in strong, dynamic utterance. Again, with the breath supply removed from the upper chest, this is left free for the centre of resonance, a function it performs in producing the orotund or chest tone.

Pure Tone. — The lungs may be said to occupy one extreme in the machinery of voice production. The mouth is the other extreme. The vocal sound, sometimes called the "middle voice," is produced in the larynx. We not only need propelling power for a current of air against the vocal cords, but we must also open the mouth — in front and back — to let the sound out. It is obvious that if sound is to proceed from the mouth, it must have room to pass, yet in both conversation and public speaking this principle is constantly disregarded. We cramp the throat muscles and swallow the sound. We mumble. We send the sound partially or wholly through the nose. We roll the tongue around and so obstruct the sound. We close the jaw and bite off the sound. We close the lips and sputter. The mouth-opening habit, in speaking, should be encouraged and practised. And at the very outset, the power should be acquired of giving an open or pure vowel tone. What is a pure tone? It is a tone that comes directly from the vocal cords, unvaried and unobstructed. The point is, to keep your tongue, jaws, and lips out of the way, and especially to keep the throat muscles relaxed. The back part of the mouth is to be opened as well as the front part. Remembering, then, to keep the mouth well opened in exhalation, practise the following —

Exercises in Deep Breathing.

1. Hands on hips. Open mouth widely. Inhale slowly by using diaphragm. Exhale slowly.

2. Inhale quickly, exhale slowly.

3. Inhale quickly, exhale slowly, vocalizing *uh* with a diaphragmatic impulse.

4. Inhale quickly, exhale slowly, vocalizing in turn, after successive inhalations, *ah, oh, aw,* making diaphragm muscles active and throat muscles passive.

5. Cultivate muscular consciousness by breathing deeply when lying on your back or when walking.

6. Take a deep inhalation, and read, at your ordinary rate, as many lines as you can easily, of the following extract from Southey's *Cataract of Lodore.* Practice should enable you to read the whole in a single expiration, but *do not exhaust the lungs in the practice.*

> Rising and leaping,
> Sinking and creeping,
> Swelling and flinging,
> Showering and springing,
> Eddying and whisking,
> Spouting and frisking,
> Twining and twisting,
> Around and around;
> Collecting, disjecting,
> With endless rebound;
> Smiting and fighting,
> A sight to delight in,
> Confounding, astounding,
> Dizzing and deafening the ear with its sound.

In practising the exercises, the main point is, I repeat, systematic and continued practice. Practice for two or three days, or once a week, is worthless. Set aside fifteen minutes at two periods of the day. This had best not be when tired or directly after eating. Even if you have already acquired the habit of deep breathing, the practice will do no harm. Especially Exercise 4, for a pure tone, should be practised daily for a long period. Listen to the quality of your tone in giving these vowel sounds, and cultivate an ear for a full, round, musical, pure tone. You will soon learn to detect for yourself the quality of your tone in giving these vowel sounds, and to open the voice-channels so that the sound is free and unobstructed — pure.

Along with the breathing exercises, and preparatory to facility in enunciation, practise the following —

Exercises for the Vocal Organs.

1. *Lips.* — (*a*) Open the mouth widely in every way. Take a mirror and look at the tongue, the soft palate, the back of the throat.

(*b*) Round the lips, sounding *oo.*

(*c*) Draw lips sideways, sounding *ee.*

2. *Tongue.* — (*a*) Open the mouth wide. Put the tongue out straight as far as possible. Then draw it back quickly, and let it lie flat and low in the mouth.

(*b*) With the very tip of the tongue touch, in turn, the lower teeth, upper teeth, roof of the mouth.

3. *Nasality.* — Close the nostrils and say, sending none of the vocalization through the nose, "I try to speak clearly."

4. *Throat and Glottis.* — With a ringing utterance, sound *ing* in "recoil*ing*, turmoil*ing*, and foil*ing*, and boil*ing*," prolonging this syllable with a bell-like resonance, avoiding sympathetically squeezing the throat.

5. *Jaws.* — Drop the lower jaw as far as possible and repeat, very slowly at first, gradually accelerating at each repetition, "We, wick, wack, walk."

All this may appear simple, if not silly. But if you have, for example, for years been accustomed to close the jaw, or partially close it, in the act of speaking, and so swallow or muffle your tones, it is a little matter that may of itself prevent you from speaking clearly ; and the only way for one to form the habit of opening the mouth is — to open it. Such things may be trifles; but attention to trifles often makes the difference between a good speaker and a poor one.

When you find you have some special trouble covered by the foregoing exercises, practise this, and *keep at it.* Do not at first overdo these exercises. Just as one when first riding a bicycle finds that he is using a new set of muscles, so in these exercises, if you have not had a full and free play of the vocal organs, you will find you are using muscles that have been lying dormant. Never carry the practice to the point of weariness.

SUMMARY.

We have seen that the voice can and should be cultivated; that the basis of tone-production is breath-quantity and breath-control, acquired by deep breathing; that the vocal organs may be strengthened and controlled; and that faults of voice can and should be cured by systematic and persistent practice.

CHAPTER III.

PRONUNCIATION AND ENUNCIATION.

Definition of Terms. — Good pronunciation is that manner of uttering words which is held to be correct, as based on the practice of the best speakers. Enunciation, also called Articulation, relates to distinctness in the utterance of syllables or words. These terms are often used interchangeably, but Pronunciation refers especially to giving the proper accent and syllabication, and to correctly sounding the vowels; Enunciation and Articulation refer especially to the distinct utterance of consonants and syllables. Pronunciation refers to correctness in speech, Enunciation to distinctness.

PRONUNCIATION.

Importance of Correct Pronunciation. — To pronounce correctly the words in our language — uniformly to give in every word we utter the proper vowel sounds and the proper accentuation — is a consummation as desirable as it is rare. One seldom attains perfection in the pronunciation of words in the English language, and many educated people fall far short of an approximation to correctness. Glaring faults of pronunciation, however, grate upon the ear, just as misspelled words disturb the eye. While absolute correctness is rarely found, one can, by attention and practice, attain a fair approximation to good usage.

Faults of Pronunciation. — As a general principle, we may say that any method of utterance which calls attention to the speaker's pronunciation or enunciation rather than to the thought his language is intended to convey, is a fault. The two extremes of faulty pronunciation are the careless and provincial on the one hand, and the unusual and precise on the other. He who pronounces for as *fŭr*, since as *sĕnce*, window as *winder*, now as *naow*, catch as *ketch*, from as *frŭm*, and so on, represents the provincial class that usually has the further faults of slovenly articulation and bad grammar. On the other hand, we have the over-precise, affectedly cultured class that pronounce neither as *nīther*, pretty as *prĕtty*, nature as *natyoor*, laugh as *lawf*, and so on. But while a strained and unusual pronunciation is a common fault, carelessness is a far more common one.

Tests of Good Pronunciation. — The test of good pronunciation is the common practice of the best speakers. True, the "best speakers" are not easily determined; but supplemented with a study of the dictionary, the best usage can be discovered and acquired. It should be remembered that pronunciation is, after all, a matter not of right, but of custom. It is a somewhat varying thing, changing from age to age, and even from decade to decade. No absolute standard of pronunciation can be laid down ; it is simply a matter of having uniformity for the sake of convenience. We have in America no one locality that can assume to set the standard. The main reliance as to the most *generally* approved usage is a good dictionary; and yet, as Professor Lounsbury states, "Not a single one of our pronouncing dictionaries is a final authority." Though not an *infallible* guide, an up-to-date dictionary is, however, reliable enough for all practical purposes. The main point is, our pronunciation should not reveal an ignorance of the standard pronunciation of common words. For example, on page 28 is a brief list of words suggested by the mistakes of students in pronouncing them.

List of Words frequently Mispronounced.

abdomen	Daniel	homage	nature
acoustics	deaf	horizon	none
again	decorous	hovel	now
against	deficit	humble	oath
America	despicable	humor	oaths
anarchist	duty	ideal	prairie
antarctic	economic	ideas	precedence
applicable	education	inaugurate	precedents
Arab	either	inchoate	prestige
auxiliary	England	incomparable	pretty
aversion	English	indisputable	principle
balm	envelope	infamous	regular
because	every	inquiry	research
been	façade	integral	resource
believe	faucet	interest	rid
blithe	February	intrigue	rinse
buoy	financier	irregular	robust
catch	forehead	isolate	Rio Grande
calm	fountain	Italian	sergeant
certainly	gallant (brave)	jaunty	since
chastisement	gallant (chival-	just	squalor
Chicago	rous)	laboratory	stalwart
citizenship	gather	lamentable	steady
cleanly	gaunt	languor	toward
column	gentleman	laugh	turbine
constitution	genuine	legate	vehement
corps	haunt	léisure	which
courier	hearth	lever	window
courtesy	heinous	literature	whole
cow	herb	memory	wound
creek	history	mischievous	zoölogy

The list might of course be extended almost indefinitely. For the most part, the words given belong in an ordinary vocabulary. Test yourself on this list. You will find that some of the words may be correctly pronounced in more than

one way; and in such cases the preferred dictionary pronunciation should always be tested by the common practice
of good speakers.

ENUNCIATION.

Importance of Distinct Enunciation. — Objectively considered, we may say that effective speaking must be (1) heard,
(2) understood, and (3) believed. It is evident that speech
is futile when it cannot be heard, although the speaker may
have a clear understanding of, and most earnest belief in,
his message. "Is not this, then," says George William
Curtis, "the beginning of oratory, to make yourself heard
and to make your hearer wish to hear?"

Enunciation has largely to do with the first of these tests
of effective speaking, — that of being heard. The best speakers not only may be heard, but they enunciate so clearly
that there is the best economy of the hearer's attention. It
is a lamentable fact that many experienced speakers, who
have something to say really worth hearing, are only half
intelligible because of their faulty enunciation. The trouble
is a lack not of loudness, but of distinctness. Mere loudness, in fact, in many auditoriums, will only accentuate
a poor enunciation; and the mistake is frequently made
of speaking loudly rather than clearly. If a speaker
cannot be heard, the cause will be found not so much in
weakness of voice as in weakness of articulation. Char-
lotte Cushman and Edwin Booth, it is said, could whisper
so that every word uttered would be heard in the most distant part of a large auditorium. How was this possible?
By a vigorous and clear-cut articulation. True, other things
contribute to clearness of utterance, — force, modulating the
voice to the audience room, and sending it out to the audience; but experience shows that young speakers need more
drill on articulation than perhaps on any other one thing.
It is the basis of all intelligible speaking.

The Need of an Exaggerated Enunciation in Public Speech. — We all recognize the importance of distinct enunciation in conversation, but students usually fail to realize the need of an exaggerated articulation in public speaking. That is, a mode of utterance partially indistinct in conversation becomes wholly indistinct when the auditor is farther removed from the speaker; one who can be heard in conversation with an effort becomes unintelligible when addressing an audience. We must, therefore, draw the distinction between a conversational manner and conversational articulation. In Chapter I, public speaking was characterized as "enlarged and heightened conversation." These adjectives are especially applicable to the enunciation required for public speaking. The syllables and words must be more clearly separated and sounded than in conversation, and the voice sent out to the audience. You cannot speak to an audience of any size with the same enunciation that you would use in speaking to a friend at your side. If you do, you will not be understood.

Faults in Enunciation and their Correction. — Excepting cases of stuttering, or of real impediment in speech, such as may need the employment of a surgeon, any one, by systematic practice, can attain a distinct enunciation. If you lisp, giving the *th* sound for *s*, you must learn to get control of the tip of the tongue, and keep it from contact with the upper teeth, in giving the *s* sound. If your tongue is too large for your mouth, enlarge the mouth cavity and keep the tongue out of the way when not in use. If your lower jaw protrudes, or if you have a sort of chronic lockjaw, if you habitually bite your words off, or have "flannel in the mouth," or whistle your *s*'s, — when you find *any* special trouble in enunciating clearly, — practise correcting it, and *keep at it* until you have overcome the fault.

Now, good enunciation involves the three processes of (1) sounding distinctly the consonants, (2) separating the syllables, and (3) separating the words.

And first, one must attain power over the consonants. An old writer has said, "Take care of the consonants, and the vowels will take care of themselves." The common trouble is, not lack of power over the consonants, but a lack of the exercise of such power. Bring out the final *t*'s and *d*'s, and do not mumble. Remember the articulating organs — the lips, jaw, teeth, and tongue — should be actively employed. The point for obstruction of the vowel sound, whereby the consonant is sounded, should be exactly and vigorously attacked, and the reaction should be quick and smooth. One student will barely close the lips in giving *b*, *p*, and *v*. Another will talk through the teeth, with the mouth nearly or quite closed. With another, the tongue is everywhere, indeed, an "unruly member." A little attention to this matter of sounding the consonants will show the number and variety of muscular movements, in and about the mouth, required for the proper enunciation of a common word like *civilization;* and to many students it will show that many vocal muscles that have been lying dormant should be developed. Secondly, the syllables should be distinctly and accurately separated, each syllable enunciated, and no syllable added. This will avoid the common fault of running the syllables together, and of omitting or adding syllables. We will not say *jography* for geography, *artic* for arctic, *histry* for history, *Amerka* for America, *citzenship* for citizenship, *acrost* for across, *genelmun* for gentleman, etc. Lastly, the words should be clearly separated. Careless speakers give their phrases or sentences as a single word. Light and dark are given as *lighten dark;* that will do, as *that'll doo;* the minute-man of the American Revolution, as *u-min't-man-o'-u-murkan-rev'lution*, etc.,

— speaking like a drunken man, whose muscles are semi paralyzed.

In the exercises that follow, which are for the purpose of practice in articulation, be overprecise, if you please, only bring out clearly every consonant sound. To correct any fault, it is well at first to go to the opposite extreme; so overdo the effort for distinctness. When you find a difficult sound, or combination of sounds, practise these over and over until you master them. The exercises are arranged with reference to the various organs primarily used in articulating the respective consonant sounds.

Exercises in Articulation.

I. *The Labials,* made primarily with the lips, are : *b, p, m, w, v, f.*

1. Both brown beauties bit the black bait.
2. Brawny black brutes bounded back, breaking the big bridge.
3. Be bold, be bold, be not too bold.
4. Hope on, hope ever.
5. The porter's parents, praying pardon, pleaded pitiably.
6. Ponto, the puppy, puffing uninterruptedly, jumped up on the top of the porch.
7. Many unmanageable monsters, married to magnanimous men, make much mischief.
8. Mary's mamma, admiring mammon and missing the man's money, murmured much and mourned many months.
9. Milestones mark the march of time.
10. Well, Washington was wiser than Webster.
11. When William went west where Wheeler was working, we wished we were where we could warn him.
12. The wherry at the wharf was weighed with whale oil and wheat.
13. Vain was the valor of the brave savage.
14. The voluble, vivacious villain vociferously vowed revenge.
15. Vivian's vernacular gives vividness to every verse.
16. Victor's verses revived a love of adventure.

17. Firmly the fowl faced the fierce fox.

18. Frugal Flavius, flushing feverishly, found fault with Flora ; frivolity.

19. Flags fluttered fretfully from foreign fortifications and fleets.

II. *The Dentals,* made by the action of the tongue against the teeth, and by the emission of breath between the teeth, are: *d, t, s, sh, z, zh, j, ch,* and the two sounds of *th.*

1. The band blared sadly, Dan declared.

2. Daniel dared to dare Darius.

3. Dora, defending sound doctrines, discomfited the disputant.

4. Tie taut the tent, and test it.

5. To-morrow try to talk truly and truthfully.

6. Tom treated the delicate subject touchingly, tenderly, and tactfully.

7. Thomas, talking trivial twaddle, tried twice to treat Timothy truculently.

8. If Theophilus Thistle, the thistle-sifter, sifted a sieve of unsifted thistles, where is the sieve of unsifted thistles that Theophilus Thistle, the thistle-sifter, sifted?

9. Breathe with care, do not mouth thy words.

10. Thursday Theodore gave Thisbe the thousandth thwack.

11. Through the thin cloth the thief thrust thorns.

12. Cease sighing, since sighs seldom secure success.

13. Surely slowness and slovenliness should be shunned.

14. Seated on shore, she sees ships with shining sails on the shimmering sea.

15. Rouse the zealots to resist the Zulus.

16. The zephyr has gone, the blizzards are rising.

17. Each daisy teaches a lesson.   Abuse them not.

18. Ezra's seizure caused displeasure.

19. James, the jailer, judged John justly.

20. Jacob, the Jewish jockey, jovially jingled Juliet's jewels.

21 Gems and jewels just from Japan.

22. The chief cheerfully chose the choicest chair.

23. Richard chanted in church like a cherub.
24. Chastened with chafing chains, Chauncey challenged Chandler.

III. *The Palatals,* made by the aid of the palate, are : *g, h, k, y.*

1. Go get the gun and give the goose a shot.
2. Great-grandfather, gowned gaudily, gallantly guarded Grace's garlands.
3. Who gave Hugh that howling hyena?
4. I did not say, wig, heart, ear, hair, and all, but whig, art, hear, air, and hall.
5. " Kill the king," the crank cried crossly.
6. Kittens cunningly crept across the cotton coverlet.
7. The Ku-Klux Klan caused the cook to keep her carving knife keen.
8. Youthful Yankee yachtsmen squared the yards.
9. The yarns of the ubiquitous Yankee used to be humorous.
10. Europe's universities euphemistically eulogized the union.

IV. *The Nasals,* made by a free escape of vocalized breath through the nostrils, are *m, n,* and *ng,* the only sounds in our language, by the way, wherein any vocalized breath is to be sent through or started toward the nasal passages.

1. No man need know need in this new nation.
2. Noisy nomads never noticed Naaman's noble name.
3. Next noon non-conformists announced renewed enmity to the government's enrolment.
4.   The cataract strong then plunges along,
    Rising and leaping, sinking and creeping,
    Showering and springing, flying and flinging,
    Writhing and ringing.

V. *The Linguals,* made chiefly with the tongue, are *l* and *r.*

1. They fell like leaves and fill long lists.
2. Little likeliness, laughed the low lawyer, that legibility and liability are linked indissolubly.

3. The wronged, ragged rabble roared ravenously.
4. The car was adorned with corn and drawn by four horses.
5. Rude, rocky, rural roads run round rocky ranges.
6. Around the rough and rugged rock the ragged rascal ran.

The foregoing examples include, it is true, many unusual combinations and repetitions of consonant sounds. Practice on such combinations will serve only as a means to an end, — an active use and ready control of the articulating organs. So I repeat, overdo these exercises. In the actual process of reading or speaking, the mind must of course conceive the words as expressing thought to be communicated. A desire to be clear must always be at the basis of a clear-cut articulation. But frequently this is not enough. The physical means of, and individual limitations upon, clear speech, must be noted and mastered. By this is meant, not the over-precision of the "prunes, prisms, and potatoes" variety, or stressing sound rather than thought, but distinct speech. We are not to articulate as if such modifiers and connectives as *a, the, of,* etc., were as important as the nouns and verbs. The unimportant words are to be subordinated in utterance, but they are to be enunciated, else they may as well be eliminated from the language. In other words, we are to acquire, in this matter of articulation, combined naturalness, ease, and distinctness. Try this desired combination in the examples following, and avoid both the over-precise and the slipshod.

1. Speak the speech, I pray you, as I pronounced it to you, trippingly on the tongue. But if you mouth it, as many of your players do, I had as lief the town crier spake my lines.— SHAKSPEARE.

2. When thou wast young, thou girdedst thyself, and walkedst whither thou wouldest: but when thou shalt be old, thou shalt stretch forth thy hands, and another shall gird thee, and carry thee whither thou wouldest not.— ST. JOHN xxi. 18.

3. And the Gileadites took the passages of Jordan before the Ephraimites: and it was so, that when those Ephraimites which were escaped said, Let me go over; that the men of Gilead said unto him, Art thou an Ephraimite? If he said, Nay; then said they unto him, Say now Shibboleth; and he said Sibboleth: for he could not frame to pronounce it right. Then they took him and slew him at the passages of the Jordan: and there fell at that time of the Ephraimites forty and two thousand.—JUDGES xii. 5, 6.

4. Nature has proved that the great silent Samuel shall not be silent too long.—CARLYLE.

5. Four score and seven years ago our fathers brought forth upon this continent a new nation.—LINCOLN.

6. From the dark portals of the Star Chamber, and in the stern text of the Acts of Uniformity, the pilgrims received a commission more important than any that ever bore the royal seal.—EVERETT.

7. In this—God's—world, with its wild, whirling eddies and mad foam oceans, where men and nations perish as if without law, dost thou think there is therefore no justice?—CARLYLE.

For further practice, read any of the selections in Chapter XIII, giving special attention to clear enunciation.

SUMMARY.

Pronunciation relates to correctness in speech, Enunciation to distinctness. The speaker's aim should be to utter his words in such a manner as to be readily understood, and not in such a manner as to excite remark. Especially should he remember that distinct enunciation is the basis of all intelligible speech, and that to attain this, the enunciation of ordinary conversation must be exaggerated.

CHAPTER IV.

KEY.

Definition of Terms. — Key is the predominating tone or pitch of the voice, in speaking. In music, as we know, key refers to the place of the voice upon the musical scale. It depends upon the rapidity with which the vocal cords vibrate. The higher the pharynx is raised and the tauter the cords are drawn, the greater the rapidity of vibration and the higher the key. Key is not to be confused with loudness. A sound may be subdued in a high key or loud in a low key.

By Compass, we mean the range a voice has, — the range between its highest and lowest limits.

The Middle or Average Key. — Now, just as there is a range within which one can sing, so there is a range within which one can speak, most easily and effectively, and for the longest time. This average range will determine the dominant note or key. One of the first questions the young speaker must ask himself is, Do I speak in that key most conducive to ease, effectiveness, and sustained effort? Bear in mind that an habitual key is not necessarily a natural key. Many people have accustomed themselves to speak in either the highest or lowest note of their key-range, rather than in the medium range. One who speaks in a high, thin, squeaky tone, represents the one extreme, while one who speaks as from the bottom of a well, represents the other extreme. Either extreme is a fault. In his treatise on *Orators and Oratory*, Cicero writes : "There is in every voice a certain middle key, but in each particular voice that key is peculiar. For the voice to ascend gradually from this key is advantageous and pleasing; since to bawl at the beginning is boorish, and gradation is salutary in strengthening the voice. This variety and this gradual progression of the voice throughout all the notes will preserve its power, and add agreeableness to delivery."

Ease, variety, and strength depend on using the middle or average pitch of the voice; we then have a common point above and below which the voice is allowed to play. The importance of this free and easy play of the voice in speaking cannot be overestimated. Inflection, emphasis, climax, and many other elements of expression, depend upon it. Now, this middle pitch will vary with the individual. Physiological conditions will determine that the key of one voice shall be tenor and of another bass. On the musical scale the bass voice will vary from say about G (bass staff) to D, and the tenor from about middle C to G. The point is, are you utilizing to the best advantage the key-range that nature has given you? What key are you habitually using in speaking? If you have a sense of key in music, — advantageous though not indispensable to the speaker, — test your key with the piano, speaking a sentence in a monotone. Suppose you find that you habitually speak in about the highest pitch of your key-range, — probably the more common fault. You must get your voice down, else you can have no strength, no "body" to the speaking tone, and no sustained power. How acquire the lower key? Lower it. Find the desired note on a musical instrument and speak to it. Relax the throat muscles and roll the voice out from the chest. Think of it as coming, if you please, from the diaphragm. Watch yourself in conversation, and do not allow your voice to rise into a high, constrained pitch.

On the other hand, if you speak down "in the shoes" so that the tone is habitually swallowed, learn to raise the key, project the tone, and get it out. This acquisition of your best individual average key may involve the formation of a new habit and a new voice. A good teacher can soon tell you your needs, but you must do the rest. A study of vocal anatomy or of rules will not aid so much as an appreciation of what you need to do, and systematic practice. "Even where Nature confers the blessing of a voice of adequate strength, she seldom adds the desirable flexibility or modulation. So, whether it be a stronger voice or a more manageable one that the speaker needs, his only method of acquiring it is that of willing it into his possession. . . . If your voice has a tendency to go up, you are to do with it just as you should do with your elbow if it has a tendency to go up at the table — put it down and keep it down by an exercise of the will. Will it down and put it down, and keep it down until it stays down without a conscious exercise of the will."[1]

Adaptation of the Voice to the Room. — Every room has a key of its own; that is, has powers of augmenting some sounds, and confusing others, — dependent upon the size of the room, and its acoustic properties generally. This key, or "overtone," the experienced speaker will learn to detect, and to adapt his key to the particular auditorium in which he is speaking. Especially should the speaker, when speaking to a large audience, avoid the common fault of a high, constrained pitch that soon becomes painful to both the speaker and the hearers. The natural key should be used. Colonel Higginson lays down as one of the cardinal rules of speaking: "*Always speak in a natural key and in a conversational manner.* . . . But how to reach that easy tone is the

[1] Sheppard : *Before an Audience.*

serious question. . . . The best way, of course, is to be
natural without effort, if one only could. . . . There is
one very simple method, and one which I have seldom
known to fail. Suppose the occasion to be a public dinner.
You have somebody at your side to whom you have been
talking. To him your manner was undoubtedly natural;
and if you can only carry along into your public speech
that conversational flavor of your private talk, the battle is
gained. How, then, to achieve that result? In this easy way:
Express to your neighbor conversationally the thought,
whatever it is, with which you mean to begin your public
speech. Then, when you rise to speak, say merely what
will be perfectly true, 'I was just saying to the gentleman who sits beside me, that' — and then repeat your remark over again. You thus make the last words of your
private talk the first words of your public address, and the
conversational manner [key] is secured. This suggestion
originated, I believe, with a man of inexhaustible fertility
in public speech, — Rev. E. E. Hale. I have often availed
myself of it, and have often been thanked for suggesting it
to others."[1] It should be noted that the natural or conversational key here referred to, is wholly compatible with a
non-conversational enunciation, which was treated of in
Chapter III (p. 30).

High Key not necessary for Increased Force. — Again, there
is a natural tendency to use a high key of voice as an accompaniment of force. To resist this tendency—as old, it might
seem, as oratory itself—the ancients stationed a musical per-
former near the speaker (the instrument used by the Romans
being called a *tonorium*), who from time to time reminded him
of his normal pitch. The speaker of to-day must learn to remind himself. The young speaker is apt to "key up" as he

[1] Higginson: *Hints on Writing and Speech-making.*

warms up; as emotion rises, the voice rises, and his speaking becomes either yelling or screeching. But this is as unnecessary as it is undesirable. True, climax is often given in a higher key, but generally speaking, force can best be voiced by the combined strength and volume that the lower register alone can supply. There is a deepening of the feelings which come welling out through a lower key. So learn to increase your force and keep the voice down in key. Do not raise the voice and rap the hearers over the heads, in expressing force, but rather keep the voice down and lift the audience from their seats.

Modulation. — Variation from the average key is one of the ways to avoid a monotonous delivery. By the relative degree and ease of such variation, we say one speaker's voice is flexible and another's stiff. A dead level in speaking is one way of putting an audience asleep. This monotony in key is sometimes heard from the pulpit. A key suited to the deeply emotional is carried also into the expression of the unemotional; so that the announcement of a Sunday-school picnic is given in the same low, sepulchral tone as the announcement of a funeral sermon.

No instrument, least of all the voice, can be well played in a single key. Variation is restful to both hearer and speaker. A song-note is uniform while it lasts, a speech-note is constantly varying. During the enunciation of a single word or syllable, the voice, in speaking, may move through its whole compass. The tension of holding the vocal cords in one position during a given note renders singing more fatiguing. In the trial of Hastings, Edmund Burke spoke four days in delivering his opening speech and nine days in closing. To have sung during this time would have been an impossible feat. And to speak at such length, Burke must have relieved the tension of an unvarying key.

If one speaks habitually in the "upper register," he has what is known as a "head-tone," if in the "lower register," a "chest-tone." In the one case he makes the head — the roof of the mouth — the sounding-board for his tones; in the other case, the chest. A prevailing head-tone is the more common fault. In such cases, the speech-note should be lowered and the vowels *rolled* out from the lungs rather than from the throat. Think of the chest as the centre of voice-reverberation, and by conscious effort centre it there.

Again, key should vary with the matter. The manuals of elocution give an elaborate classification of degrees in pitch, with rules as to how matter of a certain character fits into a certain "degree," but all this is largely dogmatic and artificial. At any rate, it is a case where the rule is worse than its violation. We know that the key in explanatory or narrative matter is higher than in the expression of deep feeling. In the one case the sole object is to get something lying easily in the speaker's mind into the minds of the hearers; in the other case, there goes with the thought something of the speaker's life and character: the impression lies deeper, and for its expression a deeper note must perforce be struck. This is a single phase of the matter. On the other hand, strong feeling — as an outburst of indignation — may often best be expressed in a high key. The point is, to get control and variety of key. The rest can best be left to the requirements of the varied and changing emotions of a given address.

Exercises in Key.

1. Test the compass of your voice by (*a*) giving the open vowel sounds — ah, aw, ō, ow — up and down the musical scale. (*b*) Repeat in a monotone from the lowest to the highest key, and *vice versa*, "Repeat it over and over again."

2. Render the following in a rising series, like climbing a stair-

way, giving the first line very low, and each succeeding line higher, let "ghosts" be the climax — highest of all.

> "Amidst the mists
> With angry boasts,
> He thrusts his fists
> Against the posts,
> And still insists
> He sees the ghosts."

3. Practise Exercise 1 (*a*) without separating the notes, *i.e.* let the voice *slide* up and down the scale. This movement of the voice is called the rising or falling slide, as the case may be, and is widely serviceable. A flexible voice, for example, will slide easily from a low to a high key, in an interrogatory. Practise the rising slide in asking, "Are you going home to-day?" Overdo it, perhaps, by using the whole compass of the voice. Suppose now your hearer does not understand your question, and you impatiently repeat, using the falling slide, "Are you going home to-day?"

4. In the selection, "Conservatism," p. 11, take the sentence, "Then at last, . . ." etc., begin low, gradually and naturally rise, bringing out the expression, to the word "hearts," and thence use the falling slide.

5. Note the "deeper note," previously alluded to, that is struck in the second sentence of the example following, after Grady has explained what "some one has said," and turns to express his own feelings and sentiments thereon : —

"Some one has said, in derision, that the old men of the South sitting down amid their ruins, reminded him of 'The Spanish hidalgoes sitting in the porches of the Alhambra and looking out to sea for the return of the lost Armada.' There is pathos, but no derision in this picture to me. These men were our fathers. Their lives were stainless. Their hands were daintily cast, and the civilization they builded in tender and engaging grace hath not been equalled."

6. Again, note the prevailingly deeper note that must be struck to adequately express the second paragraph of "Conservatism" (p. 11), as compared with the first paragraph.

SUMMARY.

Key is the average pitch of the individual voice.   By practice the speaker can and should use his best individual key-range, adapt the key of his voice to the key of the room in which he is speaking, and by modulation avoid monotony.

Key — nerve tension.
Inflection - Relation of ideas.
Emphasis - Relative importance
Pause   - Mental picture.
Tone - Color. - Emotion.

CHAPTER V.

EMPHASIS.

Definition. — Emphasis is the art of giving to each word its due importance. It is to speaking what word-arrangement is to rhetoric. It consists of any means that the speaker may employ, whereby particular attention is called to words of special significance. Such words are uttered in a way to excite the hearer's special attention. In its broader sense, emphasis is applied to sentence and paragraph relation, and to the discourse as a whole. In this broader signification, a speech might be judged by the emphasis used, for the emphasis *is* the speech. The purpose in this chapter, however, is to deal primarily with word-emphasis.

Basis of Good Emphasis. — Like all other elements of expression, this matter of emphasis is the double work of mind and voice. You cannot emphasize a word unless the mind first perceives its importance for the purpose of the thought-expression. The primary requisite, then, is a vivid, vigorous mental concept; the rest is to have the voice give expression to such concept.

Ways of Emphasizing. — There are three principal ways of emphasizing a word or phrase: (1) by Pause, (2) by Time, and (3) by Stress.

1. *Pause-emphasis.* — Special attention may be called to a word or phrase by pausing before or after, or both before

and after, its utterance. Read the following examples with and without pausing at the dashes, and note the difference in the effect: —

(*a*) The one rule for attaining perfection in any art is — practice.

(*b*) Fourscore and seven years ago our fathers brought forth upon this continent — a new nation.

(*c*) In this — God's — world, dost thou think there is no justice?

(*d*) Necessity — knows no rules.

(*e*) To speak distinctly — is to speak well.

(*f*) The days of pompous eloquence — are gone by.

(*g*) These men — were our fathers; their lives — were stainless.

(*h*) The scenes amid which they moved, as princes among men, have vanished — forever.

2. *Time-emphasis.* — Again, a word or phrase may be emphasized by taking relatively more time for its utterance. To take approximately the same time in speaking each word, whether important or unimportant, is to show an utter lack of discrimination. Take relatively more time in uttering the words that carry the principal idea; expand — dwell upon — the important words. In the following sentence, for example, note how much more expressive of the thought it is to dwell upon the italicized words and phrases: —

Fourscore and seven years ago our fathers brought forth upon this continent *a new nation, conceived* in *liberty*, and *dedicated* to the proposition that *all* men are created *equal*.

3. *Stress-emphasis.* — While pausing and time-taking are important, the most important and most common method of emphasizing a word is by means of *stress*. Hence, emphasis and stress are often used synonymously. The Century Dictionary, for example, defines emphasis as " a special stress of the voice given to the utterance of a word . . . in order to excite special attention." Now, stress is to emphasis what accent is to syllabication. In polysyllabic words, indeed, it

is accentuated accent. Stress consists in raising the voice above the average key, — hitting a word, as it were, — and thereby calling special attention to the word so stressed or emphasized. After the pitch is raised for such stress, the voice swings back to or below the average key.

The student should note this mechanical movement of the voice when stress is applied to a word, and acquire the power of applying it at will. This done, he will have learned that the prime essential of emphasis is not noise, not mere loudness, but a significant stress of the voice. Suppose you wish to express the contrast between "Capital" and "Force" in the following sentence, — "The feudalism of *Capital* is not a whit less formidable than the feudalism of *Force.*" It will be noted that in emphasizing *Capital* the voice rises on the first syllable, then, as a result of the application of this stress, it swings back to and below the average key, and then, since the thought is incomplete, it rises again on the last syllable, and the vocalization ends with the voice again above the key. The following may represent, roughly, the movement of the voice in this instance: —

"*Force,*" on the other hand, completes the statement, hence the voice falls at the close: —

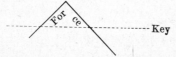

In the synthesis of delivery, no one element of expression, it should be borne in mind, is used to the exclusion of other elements. The stress method of emphasizing is identical with certain inflectional forms, as we shall see in the following chapter. In the diagrams on page 47, attention has been especially called to the mechanical movement of the voice in applying stress, since its acquisition is necessary for that flexibility which is a mark of the conversational, or natural, style of speaking. Failure to apply stress results in a monotone, and stress applied at random defeats the intended meaning, and results in a "sing-song" delivery. It is, therefore, of practical importance to know *how* to emphasize, and so train the voice to express the mental concept. To this end, practice placing a vocal stress on the italicized words in the following examples: —

(*a*) *Necessity* is the mother of invention.

(*b*) Wherever you meet a dozen earnest men pledged to a new *idea*, you meet the beginning of a new *revolution*.

(*c*) The development of *Americanism* was the predominant fact of the nineteenth century.

(*d*) Though I speak with the tongues of men and of *angels*, and have not *charity*, I am become as sounding brass or a tinkling cymbal.

(*e*) The story of Major *André* is the one overmastering romance of the Revolution.

(*f*) A life of ignoble *ease* is as little worthy of a *nation* as of an *individual*.

(*g*) A *wise* man seeks to shine in *himself;* a *fool*, in *others*.

(*h*) Americans may be *friends* of the English, but *subjects*, *never*.

(*i*) He who would speak *well*, must acquire *command* of himself.

Importance of Emphasis. — It will be seen that emphasis is a most important element of expression. If you take the question, Do you ride to town to-day? emphasizing by turn each word, as many different meanings will be expressed as there are words in the sentence. An example frequently given of the effect of misplaced emphasis is that of a young preacher who, on the theory that all italicized words in the Bible were to be emphasized, so read the following passage in 1 Kings, xiii. 27, "And he spake to his sons, saying, 'Saddle me the ass,' and they saddled *him*."

Misplaced emphasis is the most fruitful source of the sing-song tone, which comes from the stress being applied at regular intervals. This is especially noticeable in the reading of poetry, but is not uncommon in the rendering of prose. The paramount rule to be observed in emphasis is, *Read or speak as you would talk.* Unfortunately, this rule is not always, or even generally, observed. For the purpose of correcting common faults, some further rules, with examples, are given below. It will be found that these rules are largely the reflex, just as emphasis itself is, of the thought-analysis as set forth in Chapter I.

Rules of Emphasis.

1. *The key-word or words of a sentence should be discovered and emphasized.* To state the rule in another way : Analyze the sentence to find the word or words that carry the principal idea, or that express a new idea, and then give vocal expression to the results of such analysis. To determine the most important word or words in a sentence, three tests may be applied : Is it (1) a word that is indispensable to the thought ? (2) a word that a person *must* hear to tell what you are talking about ? (3) a word that can, by rearrangement, be made the climax of the sentence ?

Illustrative examples of this rule are given below. In the examples given under the various headings of this book, it should be understood that all the shades or degrees of emphasis, or of other elements of expression, are not indicated, nor can they be indicated, on the printed page ; that the marking of examples is intended to be suggestive merely, to aid in calling attention to one principle at a time, and to refer only to the particular rule or principle then under consideration. In the examples below, key words are suggested by the italicizing. Different results, however, may be obtained by the individual student, since analyses may differ. But the point is, have some reason for emphasizing a given word, else do not emphasize it; and when you have a reason for emphasizing it, emphasize it —know that your voice is obeying your mind.

Examples.

(*a*) *Time* has a *dooms-day book*, upon whose pages he is continually recording *illustrious names*. But as often as a *new* name is written there, an *old* one *disappears*. Only a *few* stand in *illuminated characters never* to be *effaced*. These are the *high nobility* of *nature* —*lords* of the public domain of *thought*. Posterity shall never *question their* titles. But those whose fame lives only on the *indiscreet opinion* of *unwise* men must soon be as well *forgotten* as if they had never been. To this great oblivion must *most* men come.— LONGFELLOW.

(*b*) There is a time in every man's experience when he arrives at the conclusion that *envy* is *ignorance* ; that *imitation* is *suicide* ; that he must take *himself*, for better or for worse, as *his* portion; that, though the wide universe is full of good, no kernel of nourishing corn can come to *him* but through his *toil* bestowed upon that plot of ground that is given *him* to till. The *power* that resides in him is *new* in nature, and none but *he* knows what that is which he can do, nor does *he* know until he has *tried*. Therefore, my text is, *Trust thyself*. Is it not an *iron string* to which *vibrates* every *heart?* — EMERSON.

(*c*) Centuries ago, on the rock-bound coast of Massachusetts Bay, one night there was a *wedding*. The *sky* was the *roof* that covered the high contracting parties, and the *stars*, painted by the finger of God, were the *fresco-work ; the music* was that of the singing *night-bird* and the surge of the gray old *ocean ;* the *bidden guests* were the *Puritan fathers* and the *Puritan mothers ;* the *unbidden* guests were the *dusky savages ;* the *bride* and the *bridegroom* were the *meeting-house* and the *schoolhouse*, and from that marriage there was born a *child.* They *christened* it *New England Civiliza-tion.* — FRYE.

2. *Subordinate the modifying or qualifying words, phrases or clauses.* Keep the incidental or relatively unimportant matter in the background, and so put the leading ideas in the foreground. This subordination is accomplished by using less force, and usually a lower key, in delivery. Grady, for example, in his famous New England Society speech, after describing the return of the Confederate soldier at the close of the Civil War, says, "What does he do, this hero in gray with a heart of gold?" The verb *do* expresses the new idea, and the added clause, being a repetition, should be subordinated in speaking. This is done by making it a continuation of the fall of the voice which follows the stress applied to "do."

For further examples in subordination, see Chapter XIII, p. 195, " The New South," second paragraph ; and p. 169, " The Triumph of Truth," fourth paragraph.

3. *Ideas compared or contrasted should be emphasized.* The thought expression is essentially one of comparison. As will be seen in the examples below, comparisons or contrasts may be expressed or implied ; and there may be double or triple antithesis.

Examples.

(*a*) A sin may be a sin of *o*mission or a sin of *com*mission.

(*b*) It is not *true* that he played the traitor in the hour of his country's trial.

(*c*) To flow with the current is easy ; a *chip* can do *that*, but a *man* ought to be able to *stem the tide* when necessary.

(*d*) Public sentiment is beginning to measure a man *not* so much by his *culture* as by what he can *do* with his culture. It demands *efficiency* as well as scholastic acquirements, claiming that a *learned fool* is no better than an *ignorant expert.*

(*e*) I could not love *thee*, dear, *so much,*
  Loved I not *honor more.*

(*f*) The world will little note nor long remember what *we say* here; but it can never forget what *they did* here.

(*g*) *He* raised a *mortal* to the skies;
  She drew an *angel down.*

(*h*) For *now* we see through a glass darkly, but *then* face to face; *now* I know in *part*, but *then* shall I know *even as I am known.*

4. *Words once emphasized should not be emphasized again unless repeated for the purpose of emphasis.* That is, distinguish between an echo of the thought and the reënforcement of some leading idea.

For examples, see Chapter XIII, p. 180, "Gettysburg Address," first and second paragraphs; p. 169, "The Triumph of Truth," fifth paragraph; p. 203, "Revolutions," first paragraph.

5. *In a repetition of words, phrases, or clauses, in similar construction, seek variety in emphasis.* In emphasis, as in other elements of expression, variety is the spice of good delivery.

Examples.

(*a*) In one of the fierce western battles among the mountains, General Thomas was watching a body of his troops painfully pushing their way up a steep hill against a withering fire. Victory seemed impossible, and the general suddenly exclaimed, "They can't do it! they will never reach the top." His chief of staff, watching the battle with equal earnestness, placing his hand upon his commander's arm, said, softly, "Time, time, general; give them time;" and presently the moist eyes of the brave leader saw his troops victorious upon the summit.

They were *American soldiers.* So are *we.* They were fighting an American *battle.* So are *we.* They were climbing up a *mountain.* *So are we.* The great heart of their *leader* gave them *time,* and they *conquered.* The great heart of our *country* will give *us* time, and *we* shall triumph.— CURTIS.

(*b*) I have seen the gleam from the headlight of some giant engine rushing onward through the darkness, heedless of opposition, fearless of danger; and I thought it was *grand.* I have seen the light come over the eastern hills in glory, driving the lazy darkness before it, till leaf and tree and blade of grass glittered in the myriad diamonds of the morning ray; and I thought *that* was grand. I have seen the light that leaped at midnight athwart the storm-swept sky, shivering over chaotic clouds, 'mid howling winds, till cloud and darkness and shadow-haunted earth flashed into midday splendor; and I *knew that* was grand. But the grandest thing, next to the radiance that flows from the Almighty Throne, is the light of a noble and beautiful life, wrapping itself in benediction round the destinies of men, and finding its home in the bosom of the everlasting God. — GRAVES.

6. *Distinguish between emphasis of a single word and that which should be distributed to the whole of a phrase or clause.* Throwing the entire emphasis on one of two adjectives, or on the adjective rather than on the noun, is a common fault.

Examples.

(The italicizing suggests only those places where an approximately equal distribution of emphasis should be given.)

(*a*) The American Republic must live. *Popular commotion* and *partisan fury* may dash their mad wars against it, but they shall roll back *shattered, spent.* Persecution shall not shake it, fanaticism disturb it, nor revolutions change it. But it shall stand *towering sublime,* like the last mountain in the deluge, while the *earth rocks at its feet* and *thunders peal above its head* —*majestic, immutable, magnificent.* . . .

Despair not, then, *soldier, statesman, citizen.* We shall yet dwell together in harmony, and but one nation shall inhabit our sea-girt borders. *Liberty and union* shall spread a civilization from the Occident to the Orient, from the *flowery shores* of the *great Southern gulf* to the *frozen barriers* of *the great Northern bay;* a civilization that means *universal freedom, universal enfranchisement, universal brotherhood !* — PHILLIPS.

(*b*) Our fathers *raised their flag* against a power to which Rome, in the *height of her glory,* is not to be compared ; a power that has dotted over the surface of the *whole globe* with her *possessions and military posts;* whose *morning drum-beat,* following the sun and keeping company with the hours, circles the earth with one *continuous and unbroken strain* of the *martial airs of England.* — WEBSTER.

Common Faults of Emphasis.

1. *Lack of Emphasis.*   The result is a dead monotone, effective for lulling one to sleep, but ineffective for a wakeful audience.

> " That voice all modes of passion can express
>   Which marks the proper word with proper stress ;
>   But none emphatic can that speaker call
>   Who lays an equal emphasis on all."

2. *Emphasizing too much.*   This fault, not so common as the preceding, is a violation of all the preceding rules, for if everything is emphasized, no contrasts are expressed, and hence no emphasis.   " Where all are generals, there can be no privates."   Emphasis serves the same purpose as the central figure of a picture.   It puts the leading idea in the foreground.   So do not crowd the foreground, or violate the laws of perspective.   A good general rule is, Put special emphasis on only a few words.   Professor Hiram Corson, himself an effective reader, gives the following somewhat extreme statement, perhaps, of this rule : " There should never be in reading a non-significant departure from a pure monotony. . . .   Great effects can be secured through very simple means by a reader who strictly observes this principle.   Every little bend of the voice tells.   But a wriggling voice, the general tenor of which is a violation of this prin-

ciple, cannot secure such effects. The hearer is presented with a jumble of non-significant and would-be significant intervals, which is less effective than a pure monotony would be." [1]

3. *Emphasizing at random.* This is perhaps the most common fault. It appears where emphasis is placed at regular intervals, as in reading poetry, or on unimportant words, — prepositions and connectives. In rendering poetry, emphasize as though it were prose; the rhythm will take care of itself. Regularly recurring emphasis we hear particularly from the pulpit, so we speak of a certain type of delivery as a "ministerial tone." Many preachers read Scripture in violation of every principle of proper emphasis, and sing all hymns, in reading, to a single tune. This same fault of random emphasis characterizes all mere declaiming or haranguing. Plutarch relates that Julius Cæsar, while yet a youth, hearing some person read in a canting tone, said: "Are you reading or singing? If you sing, you sing badly; if you read, you nevertheless sing."

Selections for Practice.

(a) AMERICA.

My country, 'tis of thee,
Sweet land of liberty,
    Of thee I sing;
Land where my fathers died,
Land of the Pilgrim's pride,
From ev'ry mountain side
    Let freedom ring.

[1] *The Voice and Spiritual Education*, p. 78.

My native country, thee,
Land of the noble, free,
   Thy name I love;
I love thy rocks and rills,
Thy woods and templed hills,
My heart with rapture thrills
   Like that above.

Let music swell the breeze,
And ring from all the trees
   Sweet freedom's song;
Let mortal tongues awake,
Let all that breathe partake,
Let rocks their silence break,
   The sound prolong.

Our fathers' God, to Thee,
Author of Liberty,
   To Thee we sing;
Long may our land be bright
With freedom's holy light,
Protect us by thy might,
   Great God, our King.

(b) RECESSIONAL.

God of our fathers, known of old —
Lord of our far-flung battle line —
Beneath whose awful Hand we hold
Dominion over palm and pine;
Lord God of Hosts, be with us yet,
Lest we forget—lest we forget.

The tumult and the shouting dies,
The captains and the kings depart—
Still stands Thine ancient sacrifice,
An humble and a contrite heart.
Lord God of Hosts, be with us yet,
Lest we forget—lest we forget.

Far-called our navies melt away—
On dune and headland sinks the fire—
Lo, all our pomp of yesterday
Is one with Nineveh and Tyre!
Judge of the nations, spare us yet,
Lest we forget—lest we forget.

If, drunk with sight of power, we loose
Wild tongues that have not Thee in awe—
Such boastings as the Gentiles use,
Or lesser breeds without the Law—
Lord God of Hosts, be with us yet,
Lest we forget—lest we forget!

For heathen heart that puts her trust
In reeking tube and iron shard—
All valiant dust that builds on dust,
And guarding calls not Thee to guard,
For frantic boast and foolish word,
Thy Mercy on Thy People, Lord!

Besides the primary emphasis, which we have largely
been considering, there is a secondary emphasis that brings
out the lighter touches and more delicate shadings of the
word-picture. Into this our exposition cannot profitably go.

It is not maintained that a mastery of the foregoing rules, and the avoidance of the faults mentioned, will give a mastery of the art of emphasis. These rules and cautions are intended to call the student's attention to some basic principles, and the examples are to afford practice in training the voice to obey the will. That attained, the mind must do the rest.

SUMMARY.

Emphasis should express the relative importance of ideas. This is accomplished, vocally, by pause, time, and stress; but the basis of clear and expressive emphasis is always clear and vigorous thinking.

CHAPTER VI.

INFLECTION.

Definition and Classification. — Inflection denotes the bend or wave of the voice above or below the average key. Its uses are to aid in emphasizing, to express relationships between the ideas in a discourse, and, in general, to give variety to speech. The inflections of a well-modulated voice — the variations from the dominant key-note — are infinite in number, but the principal movements, with the method of indicating each, are as follows: The Falling Inflection (`), the Rising Inflection (´), the Falling Circumflex (⌢), the Rising Circumflex (⌣), the Double Falling Circumflex (⌢⌢), the Double Rising Circumflex (⌣⌣), the Falling Slide (↘), and the Rising Slide (↗).

The Falling and Rising Inflections : General Law. — What is commonly known as inflection is the downward or upward bend of the voice on a single word or syllable immediately preceding the pauses in speech. This bend of the voice expresses the relationship between the ideas immediately preceding and following such pause. When the voice bends downward from the key, it is known as the falling inflection, and indicates that the thought is complete at that point; when the voice bends upward, it is called the rising inflection, and indicates that something more is needed to complete the thought. Hence the *General Law* that determines inflection is as follows: *When the thought is complete, the voice falls; when the thought is incomplete, the voice rises.* That

59

is, the completeness or incompleteness of the *thought*, not the form of the sentence or the punctuation, determines the inflection. Nothing could be more misleading than to suppose that the voice always rises at the comma and always falls at the period. A sentence may be grammatically complete but incomplete in thought. Therefore discard any idea of inflecting according to the punctuation marks.

The Falling Inflection. — The falling inflection denotes affirmation, determination, positiveness, assertion, — completeness. Completeness includes (1) Finality and (2) Momentary Completeness.

1. *Finality.* — By finality is meant the conclusion of the thought. For the purpose of completing some idea, or of laying down that which is finished, the voice falls.

Examples.

(*a*) Service is the law of life. It is a splendid thing to be able to live this life of service. — Abbott.

(*b*) The modern student knows that a well-developed body and a well-developed mind are necessary partners for intellectual and material triumphs. — Depew.

(*c*) I expect to pass through this life but once. If there is any kindness or any good thing I can do to my fellow-beings, let me do it now. I shall pass this way but once. — William Penn.

2. *Momentary Completeness.* — Momentary completeness of the thought may arise, first, from its *logical importance*, requiring a strong affirmative emphasis.

Examples.

(*a*) Then shall the kingdom be likened unto ten virgins, which took their lamps, and went forth to meet the bridegroom.

(*b*) Ephesus was upside down. The manufacturers of silver boxes for holding heathen images had collected their laborers together to discuss the behavior of one Paul, who had been in public places assaulting image worship, and consequently very much damaging their business. — TALMAGE.

(c) True eloquence does not consist in speech. Words and phrases may be marshalled in every way, but they cannot compass it. It comes, if it comes at all, like the outbreak of a fountain from the earth, or the bursting forth of volcanic fires, with spontaneous, original, native force. — WEBSTER.

(d) I am one among the thousands who loved Henry Grady, and I stand among the millions who lament his death. I loved him in the promise of his glowing youth, when across my boyish vision he walked with winning grace from easy effort to success. I loved him in the flush of his splendid manhood, when a nation hung upon his words, — and now I love him best of all as he lies under the December skies, with face as tranquil and with smile as sweet as patrial ever wore.

I agree with Patrick Collins, that Henry Grady was the most brilliant son of the Republic; and I believe, if the annals of these times are told with truth, they will record him the phenomenon of his period. No eloquence has equalled his since Sargent Prentiss faded from the earth. No pen has ploughed such noble furrows in his country's fallow fields since the wrist of Horace Greeley rested. No age of the Republic has witnessed such marvelous conjunction of a magic pen with the splendor of a mellow tongue. — GRAVES.

The falling inflection at pauses of momentary completeness, as indicated in the foregoing examples, gives the combined effect of emphasis and positiveness. Used with discretion, it is very effective. Used to excess, the delivery becomes heavy and monotonous, and sacrifices the on-movement of the thought. In a series of words or expressions, equally emphatic in theory, it is often better to defer the emphasis — and hence the falling inflection — until the last.

(*a*) Property, character, reputation, everything was sacrificed.

(*b*) Charity beareth all things, hopeth all things, endureth all things.

Again, momentary completeness may arise from an *elliptical construction.* In such cases the thought requires that the reader or speaker mentally supply the words that would expand the clause wherein the ellipsis is found, into a complete proposition. This is done in the following example by placing in brackets the words to be understood in the rendering.

Example.

Fourscore and seven years ago our fathers brought forth upon this continent a new nation, [This new nation was] conceived in liberty, and dedicated to the proposition that all men are created equal. Now we are engaged in a great civil war, [We are now] testing whether that nation, or any nation so conceived and so dedicated, can long endure.

The Rising Inflection. — Incompleteness of thought arises in a variety of forms, among which we may note (1) Doubt or Concession, (2) Appeal or Obviousness, and (3) Negation.

1. *Doubt or Concession requires the Rising Inflection.* In cases of doubt or concession, the sense is usually imperfect, — something needs to follow, expressed or implied, to complete the thought.

Examples.

(*a*) He may be an honest man; he says he is.

(*b*) I grant you that this is the true standard of statesmanship. Now the question is, did Mr. Webster measure up to that standard?

2. *Appeal or Obviousness requires the Rising Inflection.* That is, where the speaker impliedly says, "Is not this true?" or "You will not question this, will you?"

Examples.

(*a*) One must build to the praise of a being above, to build the noblest memorial of himself.

(*b*) It is not necessary to be rich in order to be happy. . . . We have a false standard of these things in the United States. We think that a man must be great, that he must be famous, that he must be wealthy. That is all a mistake. It is not necessary to be rich, to be great, to be famous, to be powerful, in order to be happy. The happy man is the free man.

3. *Negation frequently denotes incompleteness, especially when followed by an affirmation.* When a statement is made in the negative, — if we say a thing is *not* so and so, — unless the negation is itself assertive or positive, the implication usually is that something is to follow by way of affirmation, — that it *is* so and so, — and the thought is incomplete until such affirmation.

Examples.

(*a*) I come not here armed at all points with law cases and Acts of Parliament, with the statute-book doubled down in dog's ears, to defend the cause of liberty. I would not debate a point of law with the gentleman! I know his abilities. — CHATHAM.

(*b*) It was not his olive valleys and orange groves which made the Greece of the Greek; it was not for his apple orchards or potato fields that the farmer of New England and New York left his plough in the furrow and marched to Bunker Hill, to Bennington, to Saratoga. A man's country is not a certain area of land, but it is a principle; and patriotism is loyalty to that principle. — CURTIS.

(*c*) The proposition is peace. Not peace through the medium of war; not peace to be hunted through the labyrinth of intricate and endless negotiations; not peace to arise out of universal discord, fomented from principle in all parts of the empire; not peace to depend on the juridical determination of perplexing questions, or the precise marking of the shadowy boundaries of a complex government; it is simple peace; sought in its natural course; and in its ordinary haunts. — BURKE.

(*d*)   What constitutes a state?
　　Not high-raised battlements or labored mound,
　　　　Thick wall or moated gate;
　　Not cities proud, with spires and turrets crowned;
　　　　Not bays and broad-arm ports,
　　Where laughing at the storm, rich navies ride;
　　　　Not starred and spangled courts,
　　Where low-browed baseness wafts perfume to pride.
　　　　No : — men — high-minded men —
　　With powers as far above dull brutes endued
　　　　In forest brake and den,
　　As beasts excel cold rocks and brambles rude;
　　　　Men who their duties know,
　　But know their rights, and knowing, dare maintain,
　　　　Prevent the long-aimed blow,
　　And crush the tyrant while they rend the chain;
　　　　These constitute a state. — SIR WILLIAM JONES.

Further Applications of the General Law of Inflection.

1. *A loose sentence is usually delivered with the Falling Inflection at intermediate pauses, except the clause preceding the last, when the Rising Inflection is used.* The reason for this general rule is, that by using the rising inflection on next to the last clause, the effect is to connect all the preceding clauses with the very close. The demands of emphasis may of course vary this general rule.

It is sometimes said that the falling inflection used at the pauses in the following examples is a partial fall only, as distinguished from the complete fall that denotes the conclusion of thought. That is, there are degrees of inflection that will represent the various degrees of relationship between ideas. It would be impossible, as well as undesirable, to give an exposition of these various degrees on the printed page. Here again the speaker's mind must be the guide.

Examples.

(*a*) To-day men point to Marengo in wonderment. They laud the power and foresight that so skilfully planned the battle, but they forget that Napoleon failed; they forget that he was defeated; they forget that a general only thirty years old made a victory of the great conqueror's defeat, and that a gamin of Paris put to shame the Child of Destiny.

(*b*) It should be the labor of a genuine and noble patriotism to raise the life of a nation to the level of its privileges; to harmonize its general practice with its abstract principles; to reduce to actual facts the ideals of its institutions; to elevate instruction into knowledge; and to deepen knowledge into wisdom.

(*c*) So long as men touch the ground and feel their own weight, so long they need the aptitudes and the instrumentalities of the human body; and one of the very first steps in oratory is that which trains the body to be the welcome and glad servant of the soul; for many a one who has acres of thought has little bodily culture, and many a one who has sweetening inside has cacophony when he speaks.

2. *In a periodic sentence, the Rising Inflection should usually be given at the intermediate pauses.* The construction of a periodic sentence is especially adapted to oratorical discourse, its leading idea, the climax, being reserved till the close. The thought is onlooking, and the rising inflection aids the thought-movement onward to the climax. In a very long sentence, the demands of variety may necessitate a change from the general rule, for when variety demands it, any general rule should be broken.

Examples.

(*a*) Now we see the superstructure — pillar after pillar, tower after tower, column after column. . . . Scaffolding, ropes, ladders, workmen ascending and descending, mar the beauty of the building, but by and by, when the hosts who have labored shall come up over a thousand battle-fields, waving with bright grain never again to be crushed in the distillery, through vineyards, under trellised vines with grapes hanging in all their purple glory, never again to be pressed into that which can debase and degrade mankind; when they shall come through the orchards, under trees hanging thick with golden, pulpy fruit, never again to be turned into that which can injure and debase, when they shall come up to the last distillery and destroy it, to the last stream of liquid death and dry it up, to the last weeping wife and wipe her tears gently away, to the last little child and stand him up where God meant that man should stand, to the last drunkard and nerve him to burst the burning fetters, and raise the song of freedom by the clanking of his broken chains, then, ah! then will the copestone be put upon it, the scaffolding will fall with a crash, and the building will stand in its wondrous beauty before an astonished world, and the last poor drunkard shall go into it and find a refuge there. — JOHN B. GOUGH.

(*b*)   When round the lonely cottage
                Roars loud the tempest's din;
          And the good logs of Algidus
                Roar louder yet within;
          When the oldest cask is opened,
                And the largest lamp is lit;
          When the chestnuts glow in the embers,
                And the kid turns on the spit;
          When young and old in circle
                Around the firebrands close;

And the girls are weaving baskets,
　　And the boys are shaping bows ;
When the goodman mends his armor,
　　And trims his helmet's plume ;
When the goodwife's shuttle merrily
　　Goes flashing through the loom ;
With weeping and with laughter,
　　Still is the story told,
How well Horatius kept the bridge
　　In the brave days of old. — MACAULAY.

3. *In alternative and antithetical expressions, the first part usually takes the Rising, the second part the Falling, Inflection.*

Examples.

(*a*)　Is it a dog, or is it a rug ?

(*b*)　Must we use force, or can we use argument ?

(*c*)　For I am persuaded, that neither death nor life, nor angels nor principalities nor powers, nor things present nor things to come, nor height nor depth, nor any other creature, shall be able to separate us from the love of God, which is in Christ Jesus, our Lord. — ROMANS viii. 38, 39.

(*d*)　It is sown in corruption, it is raised in incorruption ; it is sown in dishonor, it is raised in glory ; it is sown in weakness, it is raised in power ; it is sown a natural body, it is raised a spiritual body. — I CORINTHIANS xv. 42–44.

(*e*)　Contrast now the circumstances of your life and mine, Æschines, and then ask these people whose fortunes they would each of them prefer. You taught reading, I went to school ; you performed initiations, I received them ; you danced in the chorus, I furnished it ; you were assembly clerk, I was speaker ; you acted third parts, I heard you ; you broke down, and I hissed ; you have worked as a statesman for the enemy, I for my country. — DEMOSTHENES.

4. *The concluding statement in a series of negatives usually requires the Falling Inflection,* indicating the summing up or close of the series.

Example.

We cannot honor our country with too deep a reverence; we cannot love her with an affection too pure and fervent; we cannot serve her with an energy of purpose or a faithfulness of zeal too steadfast and ardent. And what is our country? It is not the East, with her hills and her valleys, with her countless sails and the rocky ramparts of her shores. It is not the North, with her thousand villages and her harvest-homes, with her frontier of the lake and the ocean. It is not the West, with her forest-sea and her inland isles, with her luxuriant expanses clothed in the verdant corn, with her beautiful Ohio and her majestic Missouri. Nor is it yet the South, opulent in the mimic snow of the cotton, in the rich plantations of the rustling cane, and in the golden robes of the rice-field. What are these but the sister families of one greater, holier family, our country? — GRIMKE.

The Circumflexes: Definition. — The Circumflexes consist of a combination of the rising and falling inflections on a single syllable or word. When the rising inflection is followed by the falling, we have the Falling Circumflex (⌢); when the falling inflection is followed by the rising, it is the Rising Circumflex (⌣). There may also be a combination of the circumflexes on a single syllable or word. The falling circumflex followed by the rising produces the Double Rising Circumflex (⌢⌣); the union of two falling circumflexes, the Double Falling Circumflex (⌢⌢). Two of the foregoing circumflexions, it will be seen, resemble closely the voice-movement in stress-emphasis, as described in the preceding chapter (p. 47). The first diagram there given, illustrating the voice-movement in emphasizing " Capital," corresponds to that of the double rising circumflex; and the second diagram, illustrating the movement in giving " Force," to that of the falling circumflex.

Usage. — The leading characteristic of the circumflex is its use in the expression of a double purpose, idea, or motive. We saw, in the chapter on Emphasis (p. 47), how the double rising circumflex may be used both to emphasize a word and to point the thought forward, and thus subserves a double purpose. Again, the question, " You say he is going? " is equivalent to saying, " You say he is going, do you? " In the sentence, " Ah, I am delighted to see you! " the falling circumflex indicates surprise added to delight. In the expression of " Ah! he paused upon the brink," the double falling circumflex says, " Aha! there was a *reason* for his pausing, then?" A further use of the circumflex — a use most stressed by writers — is its adaptability for the expression of irony, sarcasm, raillery, contempt, — any expression wherein we wish to say something the words themselves do not say; as, " Brutus was an honorable man. So are they all — all honorable men."

Some of the principal words, whereby either a serious or an ironical idea may be expressed by use of the appropriate circumflex, are marked in the following extracts.

Examples.

(*a*) Suppose you do contradict yourself; what then? " Ah, then," exclaim the aged ladies, " you shall be sure to be misunderstood." Misunderstood? It is a right fool's word. Every pure and wise spirit that ever took flesh was misunderstood. — Emerson.

(*b*) The citizen who supposes that he does his whole duty when he votes, places a premium upon political knavery. Thieves welcome him to the polls and offer him a choice, which he has done nothing to prevent, between Jeremy Diddler and Dick Turpin.

The party cries for which he is responsible are: "Turpin and Honesty!" "Diddler and Reform!"—CURTIS.

(*c*)   Signior Antonio, many a time and oft
In the Rialto you have rated me
About my moneys and my usances:
Still have I borne it with a patient shrug;
For sufferance is the badge of all our tribe. . . .
Well, then, it now appears you need my help:
Go to, then; you come to me, and you say,
Shylock, we would have moneys. . . .
What should I say to you? Should I not say,
Hath a dog money? Is it possible
A cur can lend three thousand ducats? Or
Shall I bend low, and in a bondman's key,
With bated breath and whispering humbleness,
Say this,—
Fair sir, you spit on me on Wednesday last;
You spurn'd me such a day; another time
You call'd me dog; and for these courtesies
I'll lend you thus much moneys?

            —*The Merchant of Venice*, Act I, Scene III.

(*d*) The advocates of Charles the First, like the advocates of other malefactors against whom overwhelming evidence is produced, generally decline all controversy about the facts, and content themselves with calling testimony to character. He had so many private virtues! And had James the Second no private virtues? Was Oliver Cromwell, his bitterest enemies themselves being judges, destitute of private virtues?

And what, after all, are the virtues ascribed to Charles? A religious zeal, not more sincere than that of his son, and fully as weak and narrow-minded, and a few of the ordinary household decencies which half the tombstones in England claim for those who lie beneath them. A good father! A good husband! Ample apologies indeed for fifteen years of persecution, tyranny, and falsehood!

We charge him with having broken his coronation oath; and we are told that he kept his marriage vow! We accuse him of having given up his people to the merciless inflictions of the most hot-headed and hard-hearted of prelates; and the defense is, that he took his little son on his knee and kissed him! We censure him for having violated the articles of the Petition of Right, after having, for good and valuable consideration, promised to observe them; and we are informed that he was accustomed to hear prayers at six o'clock in the morning! It is to such considerations as these, together with his Vandyke dress, his handsome face, and his peaked beard, that he owes, we verily believe, most of his popularity with the present generation. — MACAULAY.

The Slides: Definition. — The slides are those variations from the key whereby the voice is carried through a series of words, phrases, clauses, or sentences, from below the key to and above it, or *vice versa*. From below the key upward is called the Rising Slide; as,

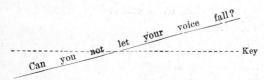

From above the key downward is called the Falling Slide; as,

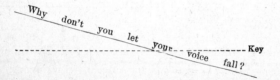

The slides, then, are exaggerated or prolonged inflections, and the same General Law applies in their use. In the illustrations above, for example, the first question — "Can you not let your voice fall?" — expresses a doubt. The sense is incomplete until the answer is received, therefore the voice rises. The second question — "Why don't you let your voice fall?" — assumes that you can let it fall, and requires for an answer an explanation complete in itself, therefore the voice falls.

Usage. — The principal uses of the slides are: —

1. *A definite question takes the Rising Slide.* A definite question is one that can be answered by yes or no; and the thought is incomplete until the answer is given.

Examples.

(*a*) Will any man deny that?

(*b*) Will any man challenge a line of the statement that free consent is the foundation rock of all our institutions?

(*c*) Is it ever true that our efforts to impress are greater than our efforts to be?

(*d*)   Is there, then, no death for a word once spoken?
      Was never a deed but left its token
      Written on tablets never broken? — Whittier.

(*e*) Are we to go on cudgelling, and cudgelling, and cudgelling men's ears with coarse processes? Are we to consider it a special providence when any good comes from our preaching or our teaching? Are we never to study how skilfully to pick the lock of curiosity; to unfasten the door of fancy; to throw wide open the halls of emotion, and to kindle the light of inspiration in the souls of men? Is there any reality in oratory? It is all real. — Beecher.

2. An indefinite question takes the Falling Slide. An in-definite question is one that cannot be answered by yes or no.

Examples.

(*a*) What can this man say? What can he do? Where can he go?

(*b*) Why was the French Revolution so bloody and destructive? Why was our Revolution of 1641 comparatively mild? Why was our Revolution of 1688 milder still? Why was the American Revolution, considered as an internal movement, the mildest of all?

(*c*) Shut now the volume of history, and tell me, on any prin-ciple of human probability, what shall be the fate of this handful of adventurers? Tell me, man of military science, in how many months were they all swept off by the thirty savage tribes enumer-ated within the early limits of New England? Tell me, politician, how long did this shadow of a colony, on which your conventions and treaties had not smiled, languish on the distant coast?

Oftentimes a sentence in the interrogatory form is really an exclamatory sentence, — an emphatic affirmation.

Example.

Is it possible that, from a beginning so feeble, so frail, so worthy not so much of admiration as of pity, there has gone forth a prog-ress so steady, a growth so wonderful, an expansion so ample, a reality so important, a promise, yet to be fulfilled, so glorious!

Contrariwise, a sentence exclamatory in form may in reality be a definite interrogation.

Example.

Charles Sumner insult the soldiers who had spilled their blood in a war for human rights! Charles Sumner degrade victories and depreciate laurels won for the cause of universal freedom! — how strange an imputation!

3. *When a direct question is* (a) *repeated for emphasis, or* (b) *when the concluding question in a series emphasizes or sums up the series, the Falling Slide is used.*

Examples.

(*a*) *Q.* Can you not let your voice fall?

    A. What?

    Q. Can you not let your voice fall?

(*b*) Is he honest? Is he faithful? Is he competent? In short, will he fill the requirements of this position?

4. *When any clause or expression taking either a rising or falling slide is followed by explanatory words, the slide is continued over those words.*

Examples.

(*a*) Did you see the procession? asked the little fellow, eagerly.

(*b*) When are you going to pay me? he asked sternly.

(*c*) Do you fear death in my company? he cried to the anxious sailors, when the ice on the coast of Holland had almost crushed the boat that was bearing them to shore.

5. *At the close of a paragraph, and especially at the close of a speech, cadence and emphasis usually require that the combined rising and falling slides be used.* The proper delivery of oratorical discourse is characterized by a certain cadence, expressed by a rhythmic swing of the voice, with periodic pauses. And nowhere is this cadence so marked as when the speaker utters his final words and leaves the final impression upon the minds of his hearers. Here is the climax in delivery. It is difficult to illustrate, by single examples cut off from the main body of

the discourse, even one of the elements of effective climactic utterance. But one thing, surely, the speaker does need to do : he should come down, like a cannon ball from the ceiling, with a positiveness and weight — a conclusiveness — that leaves no doubt in the minds of the audience of his having concluded. This is accomplished by a pronounced falling slide. To prepare for this, the phrase preceding the closing phrase should be given with the rising slide. In the example below, note the difference between giving " eternal tendencies " in a monotone and giving it with the rising slide and a pause, followed by the falling slide on " cannot be conquered " : —

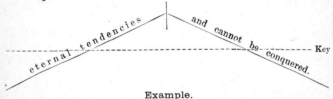

Example.

Fight on, thou brave, true heart, and falter not, through dark fortune and through bright. The cause thou fightest for, so far as it is true, no further, but precisely so far, is very sure of victory. The falsehood alone of it will be conquered, will be abolished, as it ought to be ; but the truth of it is part of Nature's own laws, coöperates with the world's eternal tendencies, and cannot be conquered. — CARLYLE.

Faults of Inflection.

1. *A general monotone.* When a generally level tone is used in speaking, the relation of ideas is not expressed to the hearers. True, in highly emotional expression, when the thought is dominated by some one emotion, the inflections are not pronounced, they are subordinated — swallowed up, as it were — in the expression of the prevailing emotion, as : —

> Abide with me : fast falls the eventide;
> The darkness deepens; Lord, with me abide:
> When other helpers fail, and comforts flee,
> Help of the helpless, O, abide with me.

The prevailing emotion in this selection is reverence, let us say ; and to over-inflect at the pauses — to use a " wriggling" voice, as Professor Corson says — is to make it over-conversational, matter-of-fact. But a large part of speaking has to do with *explaining* the thought. The inflections at pauses show the relation of the ideas. Acquire the habit of using them. If you are accustomed to speak on a dead level, overdo the inflections until the new habit is fixed. Limber up !

The well-known lines of Hamlet, given below, will serve as an excellent example for practice in acquiring flexibility. Some of the principal inflections that might be used in the rendering, are indicated; but here again, *the mind of the individual reader must be the guide.*

Example.

Speak the speech, I pray you, as I pronounced it to you, trippingly on the tongue; but if you mouth it, as many of your players do, I had as lief the town crier spoke my lines. Nor do not saw the air too much with your hand, thus; but use all gently : for in the very torrent, tempest, and (as I may say) the whirlwind of passion, you must acquire and beget a temperance that may give it smoothness. Oh, it offends me to the soul to hear a robustious, periwig-pated fellow tear a passion to tatters, to very rags, to split the ears of the groundlings, who, for the most part, are capable of nothing but inexplicable dumb-shows and noise. I would have such a fellow whipped for o'erdoing Termagant; it out-herods Herod: pray you, avoid it.

Be not too tame neither, but let your own discretion be your tutor : suit the action to the word, the word to the action; with this special observance, that you o'erstep not the modesty of Nature : for any-thing so overdone is from the purpose of playing, whose end, both at the first and now, was and is, to hold, as 't were, the mirror up to Nature, to show Virtue her own feature, Scorn her own image, and the very age and body of the time his form and pressure. Now, this overdone, or come tardy off, though it make the unskill-ful laugh, cannot but make the judicious grieve; the censure of the which one must, in your allowance, o'erweigh a whole theatre of others. Oh, there be players that I have seen play — and heard others praise, and that highly — not to speak it profanely, that, neither having the accent of Christians, nor the gait of Christian, pagan, nor man, have so strutted and bellowed that I have thought some of Nature's journeymen had made men, and not made them well, they imitated humanity so abominably.

2. *A Monotony of the Rising Inflection.* The effect is a continuous flow of words without any breaks or stops. The audience feels impelled to say "Give us a rest!" It is fre-quently noticed that this habit is carried to such ridiculous extremes that those speakers who swing into a "ministerial" or "oratorical" tone, will close a speech or address with the rising inflection. The hearers are left suspended, as it were, in mid-air, and must come down of their own accord, after they realize that the speaker has concluded. The habit has its origin, no doubt, in the use of the rising inflection for voicing an appeal, — a characteristic of oratory proper. But it is sadly overworked, even by prominent and suc-cessful orators. Young would-be orators imitate and per-petuate the fault, just as young preachers imitate the faults of their elders. Avoid it.

3. *A Monotony of the Falling Inflection.* We have seen the use of the falling inflection in expressing "momentary completeness," — in giving added emphasis, strong affirma-tion, positiveness. For such purposes it is widely service-

able in oratory. But the proper use of the falling inflection is a very different matter from its habitual and almost constant use. Many speakers never seem to see farther than the length of a phrase or clause, and at well-nigh every pause the voice goes down, no matter what the phrase-relation may be. This habit gives a scrappy, disconnected, heavy and tedious effect to speech. Avoid it.

4. *Using a semitone, instead of a complete fall, especially on the last syllable of a word that completes the thought.* The speaker with this habit seems to be always feeling bad. The effect is to turn plain discourse to pathos. The fault may be corrected by testing the voice with the piano, and make it descend at least an octave in giving the falling slide or falling inflection.

5. *Dropping the voice so suddenly or so low that the last syllable is husky or inaudible.* This may arise either from an excessive fall of the voice on the final word or syllable, or from delivering the syllable or word preceding the close in so low a key that there is no room in the compass for a further distinct fall. The fault may be corrected by keeping the voice up — or raising it if need be — on the syllable or word preceding the close, and thus prepare for the complete and normal fall.

SUMMARY.

Inflection refers to the bends or waves of the voice above and below the Key. The General Law of Inflection is: When the thought is complete, the voice falls; when the thought is incomplete, the voice rises. There are many and various cases that come under this General Law, but the point for remembrance is: The test of the proper use of inflection is not the punctuation marks or rules, but the test is, — What inflection best realizes the speaker's purpose at the moment of utterance?

CHAPTER VII.

TIME: RATE, PHRASING, TRANSITION.

Definition. — Time is the duration of utterance. It relates to the length of vocal sounds, to the rapidity of word-utterance, and to the pauses in speech. The leading phases of Time may be classified as Rate, Phrasing, and Transition.

Rate. — Rate, also called time or movement, has reference to the rapidity or slowness of utterance. The average rate of delivery in public speaking, allowing for pauses and transitions, is usually placed at one hundred and twenty words per minute. Rate, however, is a matter of relativity. It varies with the individual temperament, the matter, and the circumstances under which an address is given.

The common faults of rate are: (1) speaking too rapidly or (2) too slowly, (3) a fitful, unsteady movement, and (4) lack of adaptation of rate to express the varying thoughts and emotions. We may therefore deduce the following: —

Admonitions as to Rate.

1. *Avoid speaking too rapidly.* With the young speaker, under stress of more or less nervousness, over-rapid utterance is by far the more common fault. So it is well for every beginner to suspect himself of trying to speak too fast. In the first place, he must always speak slowly enough to enunciate clearly. Then he must speak deliberately enough for the hearers to get the thought as he proceeds;

he must not set a faster pace than the audience can easily follow. Especially at the beginning of a speech, when the audience is as yet more or less inattentive, when emotions are quiescent, and the speaker is pulling himself and his thoughts together, he should proceed slowly and deliberately. The same suggestion applies, as we shall see, to the beginning of new lines of thought. Usually begin slowly at the transitions.

By acquiring the power and habit of slow, measured utterance, — by making the words, in the process of utterance, speak all they can speak, — a student can increase many fold his power and effectiveness in delivery. When a speaker pauses or lingers on a word, he does so that he and his hearers may have more time in which to think of its meaning. " Dwell upon — expand — these words," is a frequent direction that needs be given the young speaker. Now, rate is affected in two principal ways : by the pause between words, and by the time taken in enunciating a word. The matter of time-taking for pauses we shall consider under *Phrasing.* But a whirlwind rate is marked by a snappy, jerky vocalization. If you find you speak too fast, practise taking about three times as long to enunciate your words as you have been accustomed to. Take a simple sentence, as, " Most beginners speak too rapidly, but slow down with experience," and give it at your usual rate, then with gradually increasing slowness, drag, if you please, — it will seem to be dragging to you, anyway, — only get in the habit of speaking more slowly.

In prolonging the sounds that go to make up a word, it should be noted that certain classes of sounds are capable of almost unlimited prolongation, other sounds of limited prolongation, and still others of little or none. Generally speaking, the vowel sound, which is the body of the word, and not the consonant, is to be prolonged. Especially is

this true of the long vowel sounds in such words as *maim,
eve, roar, long, all;* they are "continuant" sounds, — long
"quantity." Of medium quantity are such words as *let,
spoke, mart, boat;* while such words as *quick, stop, spot, back,
pretty,* are of short quantity, — "stopt" sounds, — and to
prolong them produces the drawl.

Exercises for acquiring Slow Rate.

(*a*) Practise prolonging the vowel sound in such words as *all,
gold, time, sorrow, glory, defile, grandeur, patriotism.*

(*b*) Practise prolonging the emphatic words in a sentence; as,
" This was the *noblest Roman* of them all."

(*c*) Repeat sentences with varied rate; as, " The glorious achievements of the nineteenth century will never be forgotten."

2. *Avoid a dragging or drawling utterance.* While the
speaker should keep his hearers close upon his heels, he
should not allow them to run on ahead of him. The modern
audience wants the speaker to move along. They may not
insist on a lightning express, but they do not care for a slow
freight. The student with a dragging, tedious rate of delivery frequently needs to go through a general waking-up process, physical and mental, — foot-ball and mental arithmetic,
for example. He needs to get, in some way, more life and
energy into his being. Occasionally, however, a student will
have acquired a drawl who has plenty of physical energy
and mental alertness; it is simply a habit. The remedy is
the reverse of the suggestions given under the preceding
heading. Clip the words shorter, especially the final syllable of the final word at a partial or complete fall, and cut
out any addition like " ugh," " ah," after the final syllable.
Let the words of your sentences be given with a snap and a
ring. Use the *staccato,* dynamic mode of utterance, with the
diaphragmatic impulse. See the thought-movement, and

make it move accordingly. Practise this ringing, dynamic style of delivery in the following selection: —

Example.

The American people have advanced from the seaboard with the rifle and the axe, the plough and the shuttle, the teapot and the Bible, a rocking chair and a spelling book, a bath-tub and a free constitution, sweeping across the Alleghanies, overspreading the prairies, and pushing on until the dash of the Atlantic in their ears is lost in the murmur of the Pacific; and as, whenever the goddess of the old mythology touched the earth, flowers and fruit answered her footfall, so in the long trail of this advancing race, it has left clusters of happy states, teeming with a population man by man more intelligent and prosperous than ever before the sun shone upon, and each remoter camp of that triumphal march is but a further outpost of American civilization. — CURTIS.

3. *Avoid an unsteady, jerky movement.* This fault is especially common with speakers of a nervous temperament. It manifests itself by long and too frequent pauses, by a terrific rate for a few words and then a sudden stop, or by any lack of proportion in the rate. The utterance moves by fits and jerks, like a horse that has not learned to pull steadily. Proper timing will result in that rhythmic movement which is a characteristic of oratorical prose, as of poetry. This well-timed, balanced movement should be appreciated and acquired. Practise giving the following extract in slow, rhythmic, measured utterance.

Example.

So live, that when thy summons comes to join
The innumerable caravan, that moves
To that mysterious realm where each shall take
His chamber in the silent halls of death,
Thou go, not like the quarry slave at night

Scourged to his dungeon, but sustained and soothed
By an unfaltering trust, approach thy grave
Like one who wraps the drapery of his couch
About him, and lies down to pleasant dreams.

—BRYANT.

4. *Learn to adapt the Rate to the thought and the emotion.*
This is, after all, the conclusion of the whole matter. We
have observed that the two extreme faults of rate are mere
hurry on the one hand, and tediousness on the other. Good
movement will reveal the thought-pulsation in such a way
as to avoid either of these extremes. True movement, in
speaking, is continually varying; as varied as the thoughts
and emotions which it helps express. We have seen that
one should begin an address with deliberate movement,
and have noted the reasons for this general direction. We
know, too, that the mind — and hence the voice — will
dwell upon the important, and pass more lightly and
quickly over the unimportant; that movement should be
retarded when speaking of the point at issue, accelerated
in speaking of a side issue; slower in the main current of
the thought, faster on the incidental or illustrative matter.
We know that emotions of awe, grandeur, sorrow, reverence,
and the like, where the speaker's feelings are choked, or
weighed down, or overawed, are voiced in slower movement;
that the light, joyous, or enthusiastic, the description of
movement, the expression of passion, as in anger or indignation, are relatively faster. This cannot of course be
done by rule; but the student should learn to appreciate
and put in practice the general principle of adaptation by
variability.

Thus, in the first example below, we might say that the
eulogy of the Minute Man begins strong, with moderate
rate; when the famous saying of Adams is reached, the
mind lingers on the scene and on the significance of his

exclamation, "O, what a glorious morning!" This, therefore, should be given more slowly. Then at once the scene shifts to the charge upon the British soldiers in their retreat from Concord, and all is movement, — hills, woods, and roads ablaze — the impetuous charge — the disorderly retreat, — and should be given with much faster rate.

In the second example, the key-word is "Wait." The thought-movement is deep, calm, and stately, hence should be given with slow rate.

Examples.

(*a*) He [the Minute Man of the Revolution] was the man who was willing to pour out his life's blood for a principle. Intrenched in his own honesty, the king's gold could not buy him; enthroned in the love of his fellow citizens, the king's writ could not take him; and when, on the morning at Lexington, the king's troops marched to seize him, his sublime faith saw, beyond the clouds of the moment, the rising sun of the America we behold, and, careless of self, mindful only of his country, he exultingly exclaimed, "O, what a glorious morning!" And then, amid the flashing hills, the ringing woods, the flaming roads, he smote with terror the haughty British column, and sent it shrinking, bleeding, wavering, and reeling through the streets of the village, panic stricken and broken. — CURTIS.

(*b*) Perhaps the greatest lesson which can be found in the lives of great men is told in a single word: Wait! Every man must patiently bide his time. He must wait. With calm and solemn footsteps the rising tide bears against the rushing torrent upstream and pushes back the hurrying waters. With no less calm and solemn footsteps, and no less certainty, does a great mind bear up against public opinion and push back its hurrying stream. Therefore should every man wait, should bide his time; not in listless idleness, not in useless pastime, not in querulous dejection, but in constant, steady, cheerful endeavor, always willing, and fulfilling and accomplishing his task, that, when the occasion comes, he may be equal to the occasion. — LONGFELLOW.

Phrasing. — Phrasing is that phase of time which relates to pausing. Our language is made up of groups of words expressing single ideas. These ideas are more or less closely related, and of more or less importance in relation to the thought. Clearness in utterance requires that these relations be expressed. Both the speaker and his hearers must give attention to one idea at a time. A group of words that expresses a single thought or feeling, describes a single event, or pictures a single scene, is called a *phrase*. To group these words that express single ideas is known as *phrasing*. Phrasing is vocal punctuation (indicated by vertical lines, thus: | . . . . . . |); it is frequently identical with grammatical punctuation, but not necessarily so. Phrase-pauses should also be distinguished from, although they may include, emphatic pauses. (See "Pause-emphasis," p. 45.)

Other vocal elements, as we have seen in treating of Emphasis, Inflection, and Rate, may aid in showing the relation of one phrase to another, but phrasing — the time-element — refers to the discrimination of ideas by pausing between them. The pauses will be of greater or less length, according to the degree of separation. No hard and fast rule can be laid down. The frequency and length of his pauses in utterance will be determined by the speaker's conception of relationships. But, to illustrate, the extracts that follow might be phrased as indicated.

Examples.

(*a*) He laughs best | who laughs last.

(*b*) Whether 'tis nobler in the mind | to suffer
The slings and arrows of outrageous fortune, |
Or to take arms against a sea of troubles, |
And by opposing | end them?

(*c*) When public bodies are to be addressed on momentous occasions, | when great interests are at stake, | and strong passions excited, | nothing is valuable in speech, | further than it is connected with high intellectual and moral endowments. | Clearness, | force, | and earnestness | are the qualities which produce conviction.

Faults of Phrasing.

1. *Pausing only at long intervals.* This is a most common fault, especially in the delivery of a memorized selection or address. Words are continuously poured out, with little or no recognition of relationships. Mere fluency is not eloquence. The young speaker should remember the old-time direction, "Mind your stops." A pause may be far more expressive than continuous vocalizing. At such pauses the mind is not blank, but is thinking for and with the audience; it is a very different pause from that caused by the failure of the memory or by stage-fright. Cultivate the habit of ease and time-taking. Pauses, as we have seen, will vary in length, but always take time for a deep inhalation.

2. *Pausing too frequently.* This is a common fault with those of a nervous temperament, or who naturally speak rapidly. The thought is thrown out in chunks, a word or two at a time. Such a speaker utters words rather than ideas, parts rather than units. The delivery is puffy, like a steam engine, choppy, disconnected.

If you find you have either of these faults, take a given selection, properly mark the phrasing, and then practise by pausing at the places marked, and only at such places.

Transition. — In the nomenclature of delivery, *transition* refers to the changes that take place in passing from one thought-group to another. It is, in a sense, phrasing on a large scale. The transition from one *completed* idea to another, from a literal statement to an illustration, from one part of a description to another, must be distinctly indicated in the delivery. The larger groups, as represented by the paragraph, require transitions of wider intervals. The speaker, at such a transition, silently says to himself and to his audience, "I have concluded with that line of thought. I now take up a new line of thought," or "I am now to speak of another phase of this idea," as the case may be. The speaker must take time to adjust his mind to the change, and he must in some way indicate the change to his hearers, just as a paragraph indicates it to readers. To accomplish this, the time-element is employed in taking a relatively long pause, aided, usually, by a change in rate, key, and tone.

In nine cases out of ten, the young speaker will either not take sufficient time to make his transitions marked, or else — what is oftener the case — no transitions are indicated in the delivery. He seems to proceed on the assumption, "If I don't continue to pour out words, I am lost!" So a new paragraph, for example, is taken up as though it were a new sentence, or clause, with no change whatever in the general delivery. It should be realized that well-marked, easy, natural transitions in a speech, besides showing changes in the thought, aid much in breaking up a general monotony of delivery.

It would be impossible to illustrate how transitions, at the varyingly separated thought-groups, can be effected. As illustrative of the transitions that occur within a paragraph, and also between paragraphs, see the selection, "Character Essential for a Great Lawyer," Chapter XIII, p. 170.

SUMMARY.

Time relates to duration of utterance, expressed by the length of vocal sounds, and by the pauses between words, phrases, and paragraphs. It is an important means of expressing thought-relations. The various ideas and emotions in a discourse should be given with well-proportioned rate, and their relations expressed by proper pauses and changes.

CHAPTER VIII.

FORCE, CLIMAX, VOLUME.

Force. — The public speaker aims to have his hearers think as he thinks, believe as he believes, and act as he would act. Broadly considered, that element of delivery which induces belief and action, is called *Force*. It is the persuasive element in oratory. It refers to the energy, the power with which one speaks. Force is audible earnestness. It should not be confounded with mere loudness. Increased loudness may be an accompaniment of increased force, but is not necessarily so. Indeed, great intensity of feeling is seldom shown by mere noise.

Since force has to do with emotional expression, it must result from, and vary with, the various emotions that rise from the ideas uttered. Hence the absurd classifications found in elocution manuals, wherein certain emotions are to be given with "normal effusive" or "guttural explosive" force, are worse than useless. Certain leading faults, however, in the use — or lack of use — of force, embodied in the general suggestions that follow, may well be heeded by the student of speaking.

General Suggestions regarding Force.

1. *Adapt the voice to the room in which you are speaking.* Proper adaptation will depend upon the physical condition of the speaker and upon the size and acoustics of the audience-room. Ordinarily, in beginning an address, no

marked force is required. In delivering the introductory matter, the emotions are not as yet aroused. Stress is laid upon a clear statement of the subject-matter as a basis for whatever emotions subsequently grow out of it. " It is of eloquence as of a flame: it requires matter to feed it, motion to excite it, and it *brightens as it burns.*" There is much practical sense in the old rule: " Begin low, speak slow; take fire, rise higher; when most impressive be self-possessive." We have already seen, in the chapter on Key, that it is not always necessary to " rise higher " as you "take fire"; but "begin low " is a good general rule. It indicates the absence of rant or bluster, and the presence of poise and control. But while a purely conversational key should be struck, the voice should be sent out with sufficient strength to reach every person in the audience. Henry Ward Beecher, who had many theories about the art of public speaking and the way of managing an audience, used to advise young speakers to begin in a low tone, rather below the normal, so as to catch hold of the watchful attention of the meeting, and then, when that attention was secured, to let the voice out to its normal strength. This plan might do for Mr. Beecher, but it is a dangerous rule for speakers whom audiences are not so anxious to hear as they were to hear him. A safer plan is for the speaker to begin with such clearness and strength that the entire audience will have the comfort of knowing from the very first sentence that they will have no trouble in following. Now, to do this, it is never necessary to yell. Deep breathing, clear enunciation, and sending the voice out to the farthest auditors, are the primary requisites of being heard. This sending of the voice out to the whole audience, known as " carrying power," is one of the several means of objectifying the thought, which is the speaker's sole aim. To secure this carrying power, practise speaking a given sentence, ten, twenty, and one hundred feet distant. Learn to get your voice away from you. The speaker must have a consciousness of those farthest away in the audience, and aim to include them within his vocal range. But do not shout or rant. Avoid all attempts at "pulmonary eloquence." Thunder without electricity is a contradiction in nature. If the thunder tones come from electrical, emotional states, well and good. But do not force your force. Remember that oftentimes the most forceful effects come from a quiet intensity. The greatest force comes from a reserve of force. The force is there, but the most effective speakers seldom let their voices out to the full capacity. You always feel that there is a reserve of power, — a repose that is in itself an emblem of strength. Such repose is simply an indication that activity at the centre transcends activity at the surface; that the motive power is controlling and moving the machinery. "People always perceive," says Emerson, "whether you drive or whether the horses take the bits in their teeth and run."

A speaker often tries to make up for a lack of thought or feeling by noise. Such a speaker needs to take for himself the recipe sent for making a famous brand of coffee: "Put some in." The relation of his vocal to his emotional power is like the Sangamon River steamboat that Lincoln describes. It had a ten-horse-power engine and a twenty-horse-power whistle; when the whistle blew the engine stopped. Henry Ward Beecher tells that his father, Rev. Lyman Beecher, on coming home from church one day, said, "It seems to me that I never made a worse sermon than I did this morning." "Why, father," said Henry, "I never heard you preach so loud in all my life." "That is the way: I always holler when I haven't anything to say."

While there is the other side to this question of adaptability, I have stressed the fault of mere loudness because it needs especially to be guarded against. *Do not rant!*

2. *When force is required, use it.* The speaker must not only be earnest, but he must put his earnestness into his speech. Failing in this, he is called dull, dry, lifeless — without force. How attain this increased energy and intensity ? Force, as has been said, is the result of emotion. This cannot of course be put on from the outside. Conscious attention to force is in itself apt to result in artificiality. Primarily, attention must be given to driving the ideas home; let the emotion and its forceful expression grow out of the ideas. One can, however, by an exercise of the will, speak with greater energy. He can wake himself up. Further, by thinking over his speech, be it an original address or a declamation, by speaking it silently, he can call up the necessary emotions, and so in delivery enter into the spirit of it. By a careful and thorough analysis, as outlined in Chapter I, he can get much more out of an address, and so into the delivery, than appears upon the surface. One might take an extract from the maiden speech of Wendell Phillips, for example, and have a certain vague and ill-defined emotion. Now, if he informs himself regarding the occasion of the speech, — the cause for which Phillips pleaded and in which he believed; the opposition of the attorney general; the youth and moral courage of the speaker, and all the attendant circumstances, he is in a position to deliver much more forcibly such an outburst as: —

Sir, when I heard principles laid down that place the murderers of Alton side by side with Otis and Hancock, with Quincy and Adams, I thought those pictured lips would have broken into voice to rebuke that recreant American, the slanderer of the dead. Sir, for the sentiments he has uttered on soil consecrated by the prayers of Puritans and the blood of patriots the earth should have yawned and swallowed him up!

So, if one remembers that Grady's speech on the question of negro suffrage was delivered before a New England audience, hostile to his position; if one has an historical perspective, and reviews the period of Reconstruction, and knows the existing conditions as Grady did, the following becomes charged with force in its utterance : —

The question is asked repeatedly, " When will the black man in the South cast a free ballot? When will he have the civil rights that are his?" When will the black man cast a free ballot? When ignorance anywhere is not dominated by the will of the intelligent; when the laborer anywhere casts a ballot unhindered by his boss; when the strong and the steadfast do not everywhere control the suffrage of the weak and the shiftless. Then, but not till then, will the ballot be free. . . . The negro can never control in the South, and it would be well if partisans in the North would understand this. You may pass your force bills, but they will not avail; for never again will a single state, North or South, be delivered to the control of an ignorant and inferior race. We wrested our state government from negro supremacy when the Federal drum-beat rolled closer to the ballot-box and when Federal bayonets hedged it about closer than will ever again be permitted in a free community. But if Federal cannon thundered in every voting district of the South, we would still find, in the mercy of God, the means and the courage to prevent its re-establishment.

3. *Vary your force with the varying emotions.* All force is no force, for herein, as in other things, an audience is impressed through contrasts. To hammer away from beginning to end not only tires the audience, but fails to impress at those places where hammering is needed. It is so easy for the young speaker to swing into a sort of " oratorical " tone, which represents a vague feeling that something important is being attempted, though he doesn't know just

what. This general fault is exhibited in various ways. Some of the types are : the barn-storming, stump-speaking tone; the dramatic, or stagey, tone; the pugnacious, bull-dozing tone ; the patronizing, "nice," "goody-goody " tone; the pathetic, "ministerial" tone. In all such cases some prevailing though indefinite and inappropriate emotion dominates the whole delivery. Sometimes this is due to non-appreciation of the varying emotions of a discourse, and again it is simply a habit. The speaker should learn to appreciate and to give free expression to the play and interplay of emotions. Of course the emotions that come during the delivery of a given speech will rarely, if ever, be exactly the same for different individuals. This, however, cannot excuse patent incongruities between the thought and its expression, such as being loud and harsh rather than soft and tender, or forcing the thought as though the hearers were hostile, rather than winning the audience by appeal. If we remember that emotions come and go, as the ideas march forward; that now one emotion becomes pre-dominant, now another; that at times, in almost any speech, occurs the purely intellectual, where little force is required; if we bear this in mind, then we may know that one can rarely deliver an address with a single, continuous emotion and speak "naturally."

Analyze the following introduction to one of Grady's speeches, and note the play of emotions therein :—

It was Ben Hill, the music of whose voice is now attuned to the symphonies of the skies, who said, "There was a South of secession and slavery — that South is dead. There is a South of union and freedom — that South, thank God, is living, growing every hour."

The selection, "Character Essential for a Great Lawyer," Chapter XIII, p. 170, will also serve as an excellent study in the use of force.

Climax. — In his *Practical Rhetoric*, Professor Genung thus defines Climax : " This figure, which depends upon the law that a thought must have *progress*, is the ordering of thought and expression, so that there shall be uniform and evident increase in significance, or interest, or intensity." In conformity with the rhetorical climax of the composition, climax in speaking is expressive of emotional *progress.* Emotions grow, reach their height, and subside. They are, therefore, expressed by gradually increasing force until this highest point, the climax, is reached. Climax, then, relates to those places in a discourse where the relatively strongest degrees of force are required. It may be found in a single sentence, in a paragraph, or in the speech taken as a whole. In the latter case, it is identical with the climax of some one paragraph, usually the last. At this point, the emotions peculiar to the speech, having gradually matured, reach their height, and the speaker puts forth his highest power in the delivery.

The climax of a sentence or paragraph usually occurs at or near the close. For this and other reasons avoid the somewhat common fault of dropping down in force at the close of the sentence. The effect is often to make every sentence an anti-climax, and so leave a tame, lifeless impression.

Sometimes a single sentence gives an excellent opportunity for effective climax. For example, begin the following sentence on a very low pitch, and gradually rise to a very high pitch on the italicized word, then gradually descend : —

> O, you and I have heard our fathers say
> There was a Brutus once that would have brooked
> Th' eternal *devil* to keep his state in Rome,
> As easily as a king.

For further practice in climactic expression, see the second paragraph of " Conservatism," p. 12.

Volume. — We have seen, in the chapter on Rate, that one means of speaking more slowly is to dwell upon important words by prolonging the vowel sounds. Now, if in addition to simple thought-emphasis, the words so prolonged indicate wide extent or large dimensions, or stand for ideas of solidity or weight, we should express this concept of largeness in the delivery. This is the work of *volume.* We would, for example, speak of a mountain daisy in a lighter, thinner tone than in speaking of a mountain torrent. So of a pebble as contrasted with a boulder. In other words, in expressing ideas of bigness, we use a big voice. Now, this requirement — or possibility — has its advantages and its dangers. A small, thin voice does not measure up to large ideas. On the other hand, a big voice with no discrimination is ridiculous. One should not use a revolver to shoot an elephant, or a cannon to kill a mosquito. Volume is a means of increased force. It adds weight and momentum. The mind and feelings must determine its proper use. But the power to increase the volume frequently needs to be acquired. To that end, take such words as " volume," " roll," " thunder," " magnitude," and *roll* them out from the diaphragm. In like manner practise giving the following sentences : —

(*a*) Sail on, O Union, strong and great!

(*b*) Citizens of a great, free, and prosperous country, we come to honor the men, our fathers, who, on this spot and upon this day, a hundred years ago, struck the first blow in the contest which made that country independent.

In the following extract from Phillips's eulogy of Daniel O'Connell, the description of Webster's physical advantage as an orator, and the illustration of the combined force and volume of O'Connell's voice, require volume for adequate expression.

Example.

Besides his irreproachable character, O'Connell had what is half the power of the popular orator; he had a majestic presence. In his youth he had the brow of a Jupiter or a Jove, and the stature of Apollo. A little O'Connell would have been no O'Connell at all.

These physical advantages are half the battle. You remember the story Russell Lowell tells of Webster when, a year or two before his death, the Whig party thought of dissolution. Webster came home from Washington and went down to Faneuil Hall to protest, and four thousand of his fellow Whigs went out to meet him. Drawing himself up to his loftiest proportions, his brow charged with thunder, before that sea of human faces, he said: "Gentlemen, I am a Whig; a Massachusetts Whig; a Faneuil Hall Whig; a revolutionary Whig; a constitutional Whig; and if you break up the Whig party, where am I to go?" "And," says Lowell, "we held our breath thinking where he could go. If he had been five feet three, we should have said: 'Who cares where you go?'"

Well, O'Connell had all that. There was something majestic in his presence before he spoke, and he added to it what Webster had not, — the magnetism and grace that melts a million souls into his.

Then, he had a voice that covered the gamut. Speaking in Exeter Hall, London, I once heard him say, "I send my voice across the Atlantic, careering like the thunderstorm against the breeze, to tell the slave-holder of the Carolinas that God's thunderbolts are hot, and to remind the bondman that the dawn of his redemption is already breaking." And you seemed to hear his voice reverberating and re-echoing back to London from the Rocky Mountains. And then, with the slightest possible Irish brogue, he would tell a story that would make all Exeter Hall laugh, and the next moment tears in his voice, like an old song, and five thousand men wept. And all the while no effort — he seemed only breathing, —

> " As effortless as woodland nooks
>   Send violets up, and paint them blue."

SUMMARY.

Force deals with the expression of feeling. It includes Climax, the height of force, and Volume, expressive of largeness in conception or description. In all its phases, the mastery and use of Force distinguishes the successful speaker from the indifferent or mediocre. The speaker should learn to adapt his voice to the audience-room and to the emotional content of his speech by appropriate loudness and volume, and by bringing out the climaxes. Above all must emotion, induced by the mental concept, be the inspiration and guide in the use of Force.

CHAPTER IX.

TONE-COLOR.

Tone-color. — Tone-color (German *Klang-farbe*) signifies that quality of voice whereby emotions find expression. Reference has previously been made, expressly or impliedly, to the leading feature of this element, but its importance as a medium of expression will justify something of a repetition here.

And first, tone-color is expressive of emotion growing out of, and given along with, the intellectual aspects of the thought. Its basis is sympathy. It is not primarily expressive of ideas or logical relations. It shows rather the speaker's point of view; it reveals the nature and degree of his responsiveness to the thought. Now, since tone-color grows out of emotional states, and emotional states grow out of the point of view, and the point of view depends upon the individual speaker, we must conclude that the classification by some writers of a given selection as adapted to a given " tone," that certain emotions labelled with certain adjectives require the " orotund," or " falsetto," or "aspirate," or "pectoral " quality ; that such a classification is as artificial as the speaker must be who attempts to follow it. Conscious attention to tone-color as such is apt to result in artificiality ; the attention had best be directed to clarifying and intensifying the ideas that give rise to the emotions. True, certain physical states react upon and produce emotional states. One may, for example, " bring his voice up in the throat " and by a tremulous vocalization induce a certain degree of sorrow. It is such vocal gymnastics as this by certain speakers and " readers " that render their utterance excruciating to a sensible mind and sensitive ear. Attention must therefore be directed mainly to awakening the appropriate emotions. To this end let us consider two phases of tone-color: (1) word-coloring, and (2) the emotional setting, or " atmosphere," of a paragraph or selection as a whole.

Word-coloring. — In the formative period of language development, men attempted to convey a given picture by imitative sounds. There are many such words in our language, such as buzz, swish, hiss, hum, bang, boom, etc. Tone-color, however, while it may include onomatopœia, is a great deal more than mere imitation. Its use is to mirror the emotional significance of words over and beyond their literal signification. Strong men infuse into their work a great deal of their own spirit. Likewise strong speakers; their words are charged with a suggestion and meaning beyond the mere sound.

Says Cicero, in his *De Oratore*, " The tones of the voice, like musical chords, are so wound up as to be responsive to every touch, sharp, flat, quick, slow, loud, gentle. Anger, fear, violence, pleasure, trouble, each has its own tone for expression." Now, it is the function of tone-color to show the speaker's responsiveness to the emotional touch. Beauty of sentiment must be mirrored by melody of voice, strong feeling by strength of voice, tenderness by gentler tones, and so on. To do this, the most that can be said by way of direction is: Dwell upon the important words, and allow time for the emotion to express itself. Take the following from Curtis's eulogy of Phillips; note the variety in emotional expression and aim to give the words their appropriate tone-color.

Example.

He faced his audience with a tranquil mien, and a beaming aspect that was never dimmed. He spoke, and in the measured cadence of his quiet voice there was intense feeling, but no declamation, no passionate appeal, no superficial or feigned emotion. It was simply colloquy — a gentleman conversing. And this wonderful power, — it was not a thunderstorm; yet somehow and surely the ear and heart were charmed. How was it done? Ah! how did Mozart do it, how Raphael? The secret of the rose's sweetness, of the bird's ecstasy, of the sunset's glory, — that is the secret of genius and eloquence. What was heard, what was seen, was the form of noble manhood, the courteous and self-possessed tone, the flow of modulated speech, sparkling with richness of illustration, with apt allusion and happy anecdote and historic parallel, with wit and pitiless invective, with melodious pathos, with stinging satire, with crackling epigram and limpid humor, like the bright ripples that play around the sure and steady prow of the resistless ship. The divine energy of his conviction utterly possessed him, and his

> " Pure and eloquent blood
> Spoke in his cheek and so distinctly wrought
> That one might almost say his body thought."

The " Atmosphere " of the Address. — Have a proper perspective of the thought — breathe the atmosphere, and so enter into the spirit, of an address as a whole. While the emotions within an address are often complex, now one and now another coming to the surface, there is usually some one emotion that represents the speaker's purpose and feeling, and dominates the address as a whole. " The whole must have that toning which reveals the spirit of the whole." Take, for example, the following eulogy of the old-time Southern gentleman, by Grady, and give it the tone-color to voice the appropriate emotion.

Example.

Some one has said, in derision, that the old men of the South, sitting down amid their ruins, reminded him of " the Spanish hidalgos sitting in the porches of the Alhambra and looking out to sea for the return of their lost Armada." There is pathos but no derision in this picture to me. These men were our fathers. Their lives were stainless. Their hands were daintily cast, and the civilization they builded in tender and engaging grace hath not been equalled. The scenes amid which they moved, as princes among men, have vanished forever. A grosser and more material day has come, in which their gentle hands can garner but scantily, and their guileless hearts fend but feebly. Let me sit, therefore, in the dismantled porches of their homes, into which dishonor hath never entered, to which discourtesy is a stranger, and gaze out to sea, beyond the horizon of which their Armada has drifted forever. And though the sea shall not render back to them the Argosies which went down in their ships, let us build for them, in the land they loved so well, a stately and enduring temple; its pillars founded in justice, its arches springing to the skies, its treasuries filled with substance, liberty walking in its corridors and religion filling its aisles with incense. And here let them rest in honorable peace and tranquillity until God shall call them hence, to "a house not made with hands, eternal in the heavens."

SUMMARY.

Tone-color, or quality, is expressive of the spiritual, as opposed to the literal, signification of words. Its touchstone is sympathy. It cannot well be described or its use reduced to rules, but the emotional content of words should be appreciated and its sympathetic rendering acquired.

CHAPTER X.

EARNESTNESS.

The Gauge of Success. — Earnestness is the soul of oratory. It manifests itself in speech by animation, wide-awakeness, strength, force, power, as opposed to listlessness, timidity, half-heartedness, uncertainty, feebleness. "Earnestness is that intense and instinctive reaching out for the part in the nature of another man which is awake in our own."[1] *When communicated to the audience,* earnestness is, after all is said and done, the touchstone of success in public speaking, as it is in other things in life.

Essentials of Earnestness. — Earnestness comes, if it come at all, from a thorough knowledge of your subject, from a sincere faith in that subject, and from a determination to implant in others that knowledge and that faith. These three essential conditions of earnestness are applicable to all kinds of speech-making, be it a declamation, a memorized speech or oration, or an extemporaneous address.

Special means for creating and replenishing the first two essentials have been suggested in Chapter I, but two points may again be stressed here : —

(1) Previous study may give you clear ideas as to the thought, and you may thoroughly believe them, but while this is essential, it is not enough: There must be, *at the moment of their utterance,* a vivid conception of the thought

[1] Curry : *Vocal Expression,* p. 254.

102

and a strong belief in the ideas conveyed. The ideas and emotions must be *re-created* in the act of speaking. Only in this way can "thoughts that breathe" find expression in "words that burn."

(2) If, as is often desirable in the early stages of training, you are to deliver a declamation, select one that will induce earnestness. Take a subject in which you are interested, and in which you want and expect to interest your audience. If you are in earnest, you will avoid anything that is purely humorous or trivial. Beware of the extravagant, dramatic compositions often found in books of "Choice Selections." Good literature only is worthy of study and memorizing. Seek something of present interest to the audience. Selections from speeches published in the daily papers, articles in current periodicals, or extracts from the published speeches of modern orators, are usually the best. If a book of selections is used, do not fail to look up the source of the extract chosen and learn the author's full meaning and original purpose. Then make the thought your own and give it as your own. "If I were speaking something of my own," a student is often heard to remark, "I could speak more earnestly." If this is really true, write out the thought and give it in your own language. If, however, the method of preparation here recommended be adopted, a student is not apt to speak any more earnestly with an original production than with the words of another.

Again, earnestness is often attained by a proper exercise of the will. Of course, the ideal earnestness comes from the speaker's interest in his hearers and self-abandonment to his subject; but there is such a thing as willing earnestness into his speech, — compelling attention and awakening emotion. A speaker at times finds it necessary to command an earnestness which does not come otherwise. Teachers of oratory sometimes find that by probing a student's dormant mental and emotional faculties until he becomes indignant at the teacher or at himself, he will then begin to speak. Learn to do your own probing, if necessary. Realize your opportunity, your power to choose what shall have expression. Choose. Realize that your will can command expression for what you dictate, and for nothing else. Shall a listless, feeble expression at your lips belie the honest impulses of your heart, which you are not able to force into expression? Conquer such weakness by will-power.

The Occasion. — *Do not let earnestness depend upon the occasion, but master the occasion through earnestness.* True, one audience will incite earnestness, while the same speech to another audience may fall flat. The atmosphere of the particular occasion reacts powerfully upon the speaker. Speaking to a small, scattered audience, with stragglers loitering in and out at the doors, is a very different matter from speaking to a crowded house. And, too, audiences have what may be called a composite individuality that effects the speaker for weal or woe.

This interplay of influence between the speaker and his audience has its advantages and its dangers. If the occasion is fortunately inspiring, the speaker will yield himself to it, and often finds himself surpassing his preparation and himself — outdoing himself. Only he who has experienced it knows the exhilaration and exquisite pleasure that comes to the speaker on such occasions, when he carries his audience with him to invigorating heights and inspiring views. More frequently, however, the occasion is as the Valley of Despair, and the danger is, that the speaker may despair of getting through successfully. Herein lies the folly of trusting to the inspiration of the audience: the audience may refuse to furnish inspiration. In such a case there is nothing for the speaker to do but inspire himself and, in turn, his audience. Not easy? Of course not. Here again the speaker needs to exercise his will power. *Master the situation:* this is the criterion for success in life, and public speaking is no exception. The speaker that cannot do this is a creature of impulse purely, and has not his powers under control.

In their attitude toward the speaker, audiences may be classified as interested, indifferent, critical, or hostile. If the audience is interested, the speaker has easy sailing. He can begin his speech on a plane to which, under other circumstances, he must needs rise; and all that is required is to maintain the interest.

Oftentimes audiences are more or less indifferent. The unuttered attitude is, "If you have anything worth listening to and can say it in an interesting manner, very well; otherwise we don't care to hear you." Such an occasion is the speaker's opportunity. He must conquer this indifference by his earnestness, — cause the listless to wake up and become aroused, the thoughtless to think, the doubter to believe, and all to become infected with his own earnestness.

The critical audience is the most trying one to address, — to most speakers more trying than a hostile audience. An audience may be critical toward the speaker or toward his subject. If the latter, the problem is to work out the best method of approach to his subject, — a matter with which, again, we are not now primarily dealing. If the audience is critical toward the speaker, he must present his ideas with such earnestness as to disarm criticism, directing the attention of the hearers from himself to his subject. The burden of his plea must be, "Hear me for my cause!"

This critical attitude of an audience, the school or college speaker must frequently meet and master. In practising for skill, the consciousness of a critic or critics among the hearers is a severe test of the speaker's earnestness. The student becomes afflicted with self-consciousness; sometimes the sense of the incongruous is overmastering; an address that he spoke earnestly, it may be, to an imaginary audience in his room, he finds difficulty in delivering earnestly in a class exercise. The difficulty, it must be admitted, is a real one, but this does not mean that it cannot be overcome. Indeed, the very fact that it can be overcome should lead the speaker to summon all his powers in the way of earnestness. There is this encouraging feature: students in oratory, while they are quick to detect poor speaking, are also quick to recognize good speaking.

As to the seeming incongruity of speaking before a teacher alone, this, too, can be eliminated by training and practice. The student with the oratorical or dramatic instinct finds no great difficulty in imaginatively peopling the empty seats, as Henry Clay found an audience in the forest trees. Under such circumstances — under *all* circumstances — it should be remembered that it is always easy to speak according to habit, be the habit good or bad. The faults that appear in the class room usually characterize the student's delivery on other occasions. Granting that the circumstances mentioned do make earnestness difficult, it is all the more valuable training for more propitious occasions. The best training for speaking earnestly on all occasions is to speak earnestly on the least favorable occasions. The well-trained speaker, as the well-trained actor, will not fail, though his audience does.

Rarely does the young speaker meet a hostile audience, and in any event so much depends upon the peculiar circumstances that directions are impracticable. The speaker's purpose is, of course, to master such an audience. He may do this by placating at first, or by the majesty of moral courage. Beecher at Liverpool said the unexpected thing, and appealed to the sense of fair play. Phillips at Faneuil Hall threw down the gauge of battle and hurled the invective of which he was a master. When an audience perceives that a speaker will not be downed, there gradually develops the feeling, if no sinister motive lies back of the hostility, that he ought not to be downed; and "He is God's own anointed king," says Carlyle, "who melts all wills into his."

Relation to Technique. — It may be asked, and frequently is asked, by the student, "How can I think of so many things at once? How can I think about how I am carrying myself, or using my voice, and at the same time think of the ideas and respond to the emotions — be in earnest?"

In Chapter II it was shown that drill in technique should lead to an unconscious habit. One should never have his art on exhibition. The highest art is to conceal art. But while his technique must never be uppermost in the field of consciousness, the trained speaker will always have a sub-consciousness as to whether or not his thought is finding effective expression. He will know what he is about. He will know what he should be doing, and know if he is doing it. There should be a coördination of thought, emotion, and will. The relative amount of attention that should be paid to each of these elements will vary with the individual. One student is all emotion; he needs to stress the mental aspects of his address. Another is coldly intellectual; he needs to stimulate his imagination and cultivate the sentimental, emotional side of his being. Another is knock-kneed — has not the courage of his convictions; he needs to cultivate more will power.

The will should also be exercised in directing earnestness through proper channels. Self-consciousness comes from a clogging of the natural channels of expression. "Forget about yourself and think only of your subject" is a common direction that needs qualifying. Forget about yourself in one sense, it may be; but know what you are doing with voice and body. Do you say they will take care of themselves? Perhaps so — and perhaps not. We have all heard speakers when we wished a kind Providence would remind them of themselves. Of course the speaker is not to indulge in vocal or physical gymnastics on the platform, nor is he by any means to give the detailed attention to technique which has been given earlier in this book. But, I repeat, he *is* to know what he is doing; if his voice is way up, to bring it down; if he is yelling, to return to a normal force. Now, this knowing what you are about, this sub-consciousness, is not incompatible with the most sincere earnestness: it is earnestness in its highest sense, for it is the method of a rational being. Emerson refers to this coördination of mind, emotion, and will when he says that "the truly eloquent [earnest] man is a sane man with power to communicate his sanity."

Earnestness the Expression of Character. — Earnestness may be stimulated and directed by the mind, the emotions, and the will, but the speaker cannot give more than he has; he cannot express more than he is. Earnestness cannot be feigned, for an audience soon distinguishes the true coin from the counterfeit. Surely art alone will never make an effective speaker. Some would-be orators go to a teacher of oratory when they should be seeking a minister. "There can be no true eloquence," says Emerson, "unless there is a man behind the speech." True eloquence springs from the moral nature. Hence Christ, who spake as never man spake, represents the ideal in oratory, as He does in conduct. The history of oratory shows that it has flourished at those times when great moral questions were at stake, —

injustice to be resented, a reform to be instituted, — and that its exponents were men terribly in earnest; that " its great masters," to quote Emerson again, " whilst they valued every help to its attainment, and thought no pains too great which contributed in any manner to further it, . . . yet never permitted any talent — neither voice rhythm, poetic power, sarcasm — to appear for show; but were grave men, who preferred their integrity to their talent, and esteemed that object for which they toiled, whether the prosperity of their country, or the laws, or a reformation, or liberty of speech, or of the press, or letters, or morals, as above the whole world, and themselves also."

SUMMARY.

We have seen that earnestness, communicated to the audience, is essential to effective public speaking; that earnestness may be acquired through study of and belief in the subject-matter of a speech, and its expression aided by the use of the will; that practice in the technique of delivery is not incompatible with the most sincere earnestness; and lastly, that the character of a speech is limited, as regards its earnestness, to the character of the speaker.

CHAPTER XI.

PHYSICAL EARNESTNESS—GESTURE.

Expression by Action.—We now approach the second means of expression, that effected by action; for while other arts appeal to but one of the senses, speech appeals to both the ear and the eye. Avoid it as we will, that part of public speaking that appeals to the eye is a most important part, and is too often sadly neglected. Were it not important,—nay, essential,—then the speaker had as well speak behind a screen, and there would be no cause for that instinctive desire on the part of all listeners to see the speaker. The public speaker cannot, if he would, escape the public gaze. His *action*, therefore, his carriage, bearing, physical control, poise, play of features, in short, his whole bodily expression,—may powerfully aid or mar his expression by voice. This, in its broad sense, is gesture. It is a " physical action caused by psychic activity." It is that part of delivery that speaks to the eye. The student of speaking must therefore answer such questions as these: How do you carry yourself? Do you stand up or slouch? Have you a graceful carriage and pleasing bearing? Is your body the servant of your soul, as it should be, or is your soul cramped and buffeted by a listless, uncontrolled body? If you have not, like O'Connell, the " stature of Apollo," or, like Webster, a " precipice of brow, with eyes glowing like anthracite coal,"—even if you have not a commanding physique, are you making the best possible use of the physique that you have? In considering means of expression, then, we must not overlook that element commonly known as physical earnestness.

Physical Earnestness. — We have seen the importance in speech of mental and moral earnestness. Now, for the adequate expression of such earnestness, the speaker must also have physical earnestness. By this is meant having the body awake. It is the quality referred to by Webster when he speaks of "the high purpose, the firm resolve, the dauntless spirit, speaking on the tongue, beaming from the eye, informing every feature, and urging the whole man onward, right onward to his object." To be thus urged onward, the whole man wide awake, is an element, or an accompaniment, of effective speaking. Mental and emotional states, we know, react upon the physical, and *vice versa.* It is a contradiction in nature for one to be mentally and emotionally awake and physically asleep, yet with speakers such is often the case. In his *Before an Audience,* the Rev. Nathan Sheppard — whose whole theory of learning to speak, by the way, is that the speaker needs only to bring his will to bear upon his faults — has an excellent chapter on physical earnestness, from which the following is an extract : —

With an adequate use of his will, an adequate knowing of what he is about, the speaker will make a right use of his physical organization — will be physically, as well as morally or spiritually, in earnest. . . . We are always to bear in mind that an impression is produced by the speaker quite apart from and often in spite of the words he utters. It is a mesmeric influence, it is feeling, reflection, thought produced by the animal galvanic battery on two legs. . . . Never allow yourself to go physically to sleep if you expect to keep yourself mentally awake.

A good preacher once asked me what I thought he needed most to make his speaking more effective. " Put one thing into your style," I said, " and I'll let you off." " What is that ? '

" Vivacity." He had an excellent bass voice and unexceptional manners, but he was monotonously orotund, and getting more and more so. Vivacity would improve his oratory and prolong his pastorate. He could secure it, not by forgetting himself and thinking only of his subject, — that he had done for twenty years, — or by five-dollar lessons in imitative elocution, — those he had tried to his cost, — he could secure vivacity by willing it into his style. The way to be vivacious is to be vivacious. The education is all done upon one side of the man, — the intellectual side, — and it fails from not getting something in the way of " earnest " education on the physical side, — the outside, — which it is the fashion to look upon as the lower side. . . .

Straighten up and keep yourself straight. Walk upright. The " shoulder-braces " are of no use except to suggest bracing yourself up. They will not keep your shoulders back, but they will make *you* keep your shoulders back. They jog the will. When you straighten up for the first time you will find that your clothes do not fit you. . . . This physical discipline will suggest and promote physical self-respect, and that in turn will promote moral self-respect. The attitude of dignity dignifies the feeling. Straightening the spine stiffens the moral vertebra. The self-distrustful speaker is helped by a confident demeanor. Try it.

True physical earnestness is something more than physical energy. Such energy must be held in proper reserve and directed by the will. When so held and directed, it becomes physical control; and just as the highest form of earnestness is self-control, so the highest form of physical earnestness is physical control. It will depend upon the individual as to whether he needs physical excitation or repression. To check energy is, however, always easier than to excite it. It is therefore best, as a general rule, to give enthusiasm vent and cut loose. " Something may come of this, whereas nothing can come from doing nothing;" and "no man," says Edward Everett Hale, " will ever become a speaker until he is willing to make a fool of himself for the sake of his subject."

Let us see some of the ways in which physical earnestness manifests itself in the act of speaking.

The Expression of Physical Earnestness.

1. *Approaching the Audience.* The moment that you rise to walk upon the platform, or to step out before the audience, as the case may be, you begin to speak — with the body. Self-mastery and self-poise at this point will go far toward winning your audience. In this position, what do you most need? First and foremost, the right mental attitude toward the audience. What is that? First, realize the importance of the occasion, — for any occasion is important that calls a number of persons to hear you speak: you should therefore be dignified. Secondly, being prepared with something that you very much want to say to that audience, you are interested in the subject-matter of your speech: you will therefore show this interest by a direct, businesslike, animated carriage. Thirdly, common courtesy will impel you to be thankful to the audience for this opportunity to deliver your message: therefore your bearing will be deferential. With such a mental attitude toward your subject and the occasion, you will bow respectfully to the presiding officer, if there be one, and walk easily and directly to where you begin speaking. This walk should be neither a mincing step nor a stride; neither the walk of a soldier on the march, nor the shuffling gait of the aged and infirm; nor should it be a sort of a catlike tread taken by speakers who seem to be trying to approach the audience unobserved. It should be that easy, dignified, upright walk that denotes that the speaker knows what he is there for, and is not making any fuss over getting to the proper place for speaking. He stops and — bows? That depends upon the formality of the occasion, or the amount of "enthusiastic applause"

that greets him.   Nowadays the bow to the audience is often given only at the close — a bow of thanks, on retiring — in token of the speaker's appreciation.   But in any event, look about at your audience for a moment, thus asking their attention to what you have to say.   Accustom yourself to look calmly and directly at the audience; this is half of the battle at this point.   If control is difficult, take a deep breath before beginning to speak.   Assume an attitude of physical ease; and having taken that position, do not shuffle the feet.   You are told to stand so that "a plumb-line dropped from the chin would pass through the heel of the left foot;" but realize your business and your dignity, and never mind the plumb-line.   Stand up! the hips thrown back, the chest forward, representing the Delsarte principle of "strength in repose."   This erect position, with the body easily poised, is the natural position in the "repose" of the public speaker.   It signifies earnestness and the serenity of conscious power.   Begin speaking deliberately, easily, and clearly.   After talking a moment to one portion of the audience, turn and speak to another portion.

This much, together with some simple directions that follow later, may properly be said to the beginner; but beware of directions for "toeing a line" and measuring the proper "angle between the feet," for the speaker's carriage cannot be assumed by rule.   It results from the mental attitude and one's all-round physical training.

2. *Carriage*.   The normal, fair-weather attitude that characterizes an easy and graceful carriage has been described above.   For the most part the body is left in easy poise, so the weight may be easily shifted from one foot to the other.   As has been said, much depends upon the mind.   Cultivate the feeling of ease, and let the carriage adjust itself to this feeling.   This adjustment to a feeling of easy poise will keep you from straddling, or standing rigid

as though the feet were glued to the floor and the knees had no joints in them, or swaying the body constantly from one foot to the other, or sagging down on one hip.

Along with the acquirement of this easy poise, form the habit from the outset of letting the arms and hands hang easily at your side. This may seem awkward at first. You are apt to be painfully conscious of these appendages, and the first impulse is to get them out of the way. But by compelling yourself to let your arms and hands go, an unconsciousness of them will in time come that will never come from trying to do something else with them. Do not fold them behind the back or in front of you; do not dig them into your clothing; do not employ them in fumbling your watch chain or adjusting your cuffs; and, above all, do not thrust them into your pockets, — it is not dignified, and is a signal of nervousness to the audience.

The importance of a speaker's bearing cannot be over-estimated. We know the importance in conversation of a pleasing bearing, of an animated and mobile facial expression. It is quite as important in the enlarged and heightened conversation of public speech. How an arrogant, conceited bearing repels, and a sympathetic, modest, deferential bearing attracts! How an uncertain bearing disturbs, and how a confident bearing imparts ease to the audience! Now, here again it should be borne in mind that bearing, as a phase of physical expression, is — or should be — the outward manifestation of inward states. We must therefore set aright the inward states. What should be the proper mental attitude that is indicated by one's bearing? First, since public speaking has for its primary purpose the communication of thought, the speaker should consciously assume and maintain the *communicative* attitude. Such a mental attitude will result in the physical attitude of *directness*. Face your audience squarely. Do not speak over one shoulder. Do not look at the floor, or at the ceiling, or out of the window, or anywhere but at the audience. This habit, trying in conversation, is exasperating in public speaking. Your business is with your audience, and it is your business to make them realize this fact. Moreover, to look directly at your audience is one of the best cures for stage-fright, for it takes the speaker's attention from himself and puts it where it should be — on getting the thought from his own mind into the minds of his hearers. In doing this the eyes are constantly saying to the hearers, "I am speaking to you, and you, and you." Now, this does not mean singling out any individual in the sense of recognizing him, but it means keeping the audience within the range of vision. In this connection, avoid showing a partiality for one group of hearers to the exclusion of others. Look about, while looking at, the audience. Do not shift the eyes capriciously, but do it deliberately and easily, as the natural thing to do. And turn the body with the eyes, — not the head alone, nor the trunk alone, but the whole body.

Rarely should the speaker's eyes leave the audience. The actor talks with others on the stage, the public speaker carries on a one-sided dialogue with the audience only. The actor may occasionally even turn his back to the audience; the public speaker, never. True, he may at times, in picturing a scene or describing an object, turn the eyes momentarily from the audience, but only momentarily. In such a case the eyes play back and forth from the picture or object to the audience, and are all the time saying, Do you see it? The impersonation of the actor or dramatic reader is rarely to be employed by the public speaker. To turn away at any length from the audience indicates a wrong mental attitude and is apt to give the impression of artificiality. The speaker who has and maintains the communicative attitude will speak *to*, not before, his audience. He will *objectify* his thought, not soliloquize. He will centre his attention in his audience, not in himself. Further, such an attitude will be characterized by good will toward his audience. The speaker takes the audience into his confidence. This in turn inspires confidence on the part of the audience, and a mutual sympathy is established. Thus will result a bearing deferential though dignified, confiding though confident. Thus the speaker's bearing becomes an important aspect of physical earnestness.

This communicative attitude being taken, this sympathetic relation between yourself and your audience being established, do nothing to destroy or mar it. Herein the instruction must be largely negative. No one can or should, in the act of speaking, be giving his chief attention to this or that peccadillo regarding his carriage or bearing, but certain common bad habits should receive attention and be willed out of one's speaking. The point is, every movement that a speaker makes means — or should mean — something. Hence avoid indulging in movements which are purely habit and which mean nothing. One will naturally move the body slightly, as we have seen, as he turns from one portion of the audience to another. He will move still more, stepping backward or forward (not hitching sideways), at his transitions. But do not be constantly moving; it makes the audience also restless. Do not walk back and forth along the edge of the platform like a caged lion. Do not shrug your shoulders, or twist your mouth, or make faces. Note how the water-drinking or handkerchief habit will distract the attention of an audience; the thought is, when will the speaker take another drink or next grasp his handkerchief? If the distracting cause is beyond the speaker's control, circumstances must of course determine the course of action, but the mistake is often made of attempting to ignore things that an audience will not ignore. During the opening song at a recent church service the minister dropped his glasses. He began preaching extemporaneously, presently started to consult his notes, and then seemed first to miss the glasses. He kept on slowly with the introductory exegesis of his text, meanwhile on a still hunt for the glasses. He raised the Bible — not there. He felt in all his pockets. He scanned the floor, and finally saw where they had fallen. Then he gradually edged toward them — all the while speaking — and finally, at the end of a long sentence, dove down and brought them up, like a fish-hawk his prey, and the congregation breathed a common sigh of relief. The preacher's composure was more admirable than his judgment. Before the search had proceeded far, the whole congregation had forsaken the sermon and joined in the search for the glasses. It would have been far better to have stopped, hunted up the glasses, and then proceeded with the sermon. So, if a window is to be opened or closed, or a dog removed, let the speaker, when possible, join the audience in watching the proceeding, and then proceed with the speech.

Gesture. — If the speaker be physically in earnest, what is commonly known as gesture should not seriously trouble him. Reference is now made to gesture in its narrower sense, the use of the arms and hands as an aid in emphasizing or suggesting the thought. There has probably been more nonsense written about gesture in manuals of elocution than about any other one thing connected with delivery. We are told, for example, that this or that mental or emotional state is represented by " hand supine " or " hand prone." The body is divided into " spheres " or " zones," and we are told that gestures made below the waist line denote the lower passions, and those above the shoulder the higher passions. Elaborate charts are given to indicate the action of various parts of the body in expressing various emotions. In such a chart, prepared by the professor of oratory in a prominent Eastern university, forty-four emotions are listed. We are told, for example, that "Appeal to Conscience" is indicated by "head thrown forward, eyes and brows looking forward, lips and countenance earnest, trunk erect, one hand on breast, lower limbs erect, movements slow." Now there are two palpable objections to this sort of instruction: first, the assumption that a given emotion will naturally be expressed by every individual in the same way or in a given "sphere," is not true; second, if there were some truth in the underlying principles presented, all these directions are bound to produce mechanical and artificial results.

And yet the problem remains. Gestures, used sparingly and effectively, are a powerful aid to public speech. They constitute our sign-language. They are used much more freely by some individuals than by others; yet any speaker, if he is awake, if he is physically in earnest, will at times in the relatively stronger utterance, feel an impulse to use his arms and hands to emphasize or illustrate his thought. And the problem is, to see to it that these movements of the arms and hands work themselves out along graceful and effective lines. It is a problem in economy of muscular energy, in the union of action and repose, and in the coordination of physical energy with mental and emotional energy. General preparation must therefore be made in an all-round physical training. Playing tennis, dancing, swinging Indian clubs and dumb-bells, gymnasium exercise, — especially the free movements of the "Swedish System" — are all excellent for acquiring muscular control and relaxation. If a gymnasium is accessible, by all means use it, and let a physical expert prescribe for you. The first effort of the student usually needs to be directed toward limbering up his arms and body, avoiding all rigidity, and cultivating a passive or elastic state. For the benefit of those who may not have access to a gymnasium, a few simple calisthenics are appended which, if regularly and faithfully practised, will be found helpful, especially in getting a desired relaxation of the arms and hands.

Calisthenics Preparatory to Gesture.

1. Stand erect, chest prominent, body in easy poise.

2. Dangle the hands, and shake the arms freely from the shoulders, (*a*) at the side, (*b*) held horizontally in front, and (*c*) horizontally at the side.

3. Rotate the body on the hip-joints, letting the arms and hands swing freely. Begin slowly, turning the trunk and head as much as possible, then gradually accelerate until the movement is as rapid and energetic as possible.

4. Raise the upper arm slightly, the fore-arm and hand trailing. Now unfold the arm and hand by consciously vitalizing in turn the fore-arm, wrist, palm, fingers, the hand opening at about the level of the hips and midway between the front and side. Practise this with the right arm and hand, then the left, then both together.

5. The same as 4, except that the hands are to be unfolded at about the level of the shoulders.

6. Practise the foregoing unfolding movement, first with one arm and hand, and then with both together, the hands unfolding directly in front at first; then, in succession, during five or six repetitions, end the movement at varying angles between the front and the side.

7. Imagine you are raising a pound ball held in the palm of the hand; raise it to a level with the head, then cast it down, letting it roll out of the palm and over the fingers.

We shall presently see the practical use of these exercises. In practising, cultivate muscular consciousness, and have the mind work in coördination with the prescribed movement, — active when action is prescribed, at ease when relaxation is desired.

The Mechanics of Gesture. — Just how much attention should be called to mechanics in gesture, is a mooted question with teachers; but this, again, depends upon the individual. Certainly no one wants to become a "looking-glass orator," but in the process of preliminary training and practice, the young speaker may well turn his attention and his will, if need be, upon his arm and hand movements, even to watching himself before a large mirror, and note whether or not he is making these movements along graceful and expressive lines. Now, any gesture may be analyzed into the movements (*a*) of preparation and (*b*) of execution, or stroke. Let us see how this works out in a given gesture. Suppose you want to emphasize by gesture the negation expressed in the following: "You say that we are weak; but I say that we are *not* weak, if we make a proper use of our God-given powers." You are to emphasize *not*. Beginning with the second clause, you have this purpose in mind; this purpose is indicated by raising the arm and hand, the elbow and fingers slightly bent — not rigid, yet alive — the arm descending with a vigorous stroke on *not*. The culmination of this stroke is marked by a straightening of the arm, hand, and fingers (though not stiffly), the impulse going out through the tips of the fingers. Remember that the impulse is to be sent out to the audience, and not lodged in the elbow or wrist, with a resulting lifeless hand. The hand should be opened toward the audience, — palm, thumb, and fingers — neither perpendicularly nor horizontally, neither rigid nor lifeless. Try to feel the impulse to the very finger-tips, and hold the hand there a moment until the impulse is spent, then allow the arm to come back

easily to the side.   Try this, first one hand, then the other,
then both together, aiming to economize muscular energy
by avoiding all rigidity.

Gestures Classified. — For the purposes of the public
speaker, gestures may be classified as *Emphatic, Suggestive,*
and *Locative.*   These terms are largely self-defining.

The *Emphatic gesture* is most commonly used by the public speaker.   It aids the vocal emphasis, and indicates strong
mental or moral earnestness.   The illustration used above
would be an emphatic gesture.   The emotional force, it
should be noted, will determine the length of the sweep on
the preparatory movement and the vigor of the stroke.   Any
gesture, to be expressive, must be neither lifeless on the one
hand nor over-elaborate or jerky on the other.   Many of the
most expressive emphatic gestures are made with a slight
movement of the arm near the hips, — the easy, offhand
colloquial gesture.   This was a characteristic gesture with
Wendell Phillips, and made so unobtrusively that contemporaries differed as to the frequency of his gestures, some
testifying that he used many, others claiming that he made
very few.   The lesson is, his gestures, *as gestures*, made no
impression upon the audience.

The *Suggestive gesture* might also be termed the gesture
of description.   Its use is to stimulate the imagination, first
of the speaker and then of the audience, in more clearly
perceiving objects or scenes spoken of, but not present to
the view.   You see the object or scene, you want the audience
to see it.   The vividness with which you see it will determine in the first instance your ability to make your audience
see it.   Now, if your audience is to share in your mental
picture, you must place the picture where the audience can
see it with you, not back of you, nor too far to one side.
The eyes will precede the gesture, and will play back and

forth (as previously suggested) from the picture to the audience. The gesture will not mark the object or scene described by metes and bounds: it is suggestive merely.

Another point to be remembered: *Be consistent in description.* If, for example, you are describing a battle, you place the cavalry on one side here, the infantry there, the enemy over yonder. In the progress of the battle you will not have one army move now one way, now another, nor have the cavalry on one side charge upon its own infantry.

The suggestive gesture is widely serviceable, yet it is often much overworked. It is a good plan to present many things directly to the imagination of the audience without seeking the aid of gesture.

The *Locative gesture* is used to point out or refer to persons or objects that may be actually seen by the audience. If a lawyer in the court room says, "There sits my client," or a speaker asks, "Do you see that tree standing yonder?" the locative gesture would naturally be used. When the statue of the Minute Man of the Revolution was unveiled at Concord, Mr. Curtis said, in the course of his oration (addressing the statue), "But should we or our descendants, false to justice and humanity, betray in any way your cause, spring into life, as a hundred years ago, descend and lead us, as God led you in saving America, to save the hopes of man." Now, when invoking the spirit of the Minute Man, the speaker must have used a locative gesture of some sort; it may have been with the eyes only. It is apparent that if this passage occurred in a declamation (unless the speaker were in sight of the statue), the gesture becomes suggestive merely. The general principle is, then, do not look at any object or scene, real or imaginary, at any length, unless you want the audience to look there too. If they are really following you, they will follow your look.

The foregoing classes of gestures are variously combined.

For example, the use of the index-finger in close reasoning is a combination of the suggestive and emphatic; as, "The point I make is this." So also, the arms extended, denoting breadth of ideas, or extent; as, "Everywhere, spread all over in characters of living light, let there be inscribed that other sentiment, dear to every true American heart, Liberty and Union." Again, the gesture of appeal, single or double, is a combination of the locative and emphatic, locating those appealed to, and at the same emphasizing the idea or senti-ment; as, "I appeal to you, fellow-students, to make this institution all that it should be as an influence in this com-monwealth."

General Principles of Gesture.

1. *Gesture should be made from the chest as a centre.* The impulse should go from the speaker out through the arm to the audience. The upper arm should lead, as we have seen, followed more or less quickly by the fore-arm, wrist, and hand. This done, there will result a free arm movement that should characterize even the most colloquial gesture. Avoid starting the impulse at the wrist, or at the elbow, with the upper arm hugging the body.

2. *The curve is the line of grace and beauty.* The Greeks long ago discovered this truth. Angular movements are awkward. Gestures should therefore, generally speaking, be made along curved lines. In the preparatory movement there is the folding-up, and in the stroke the unfolding, of the arm and hand, not like a jack-knife, but in a spiral movement, like the snapping of a limber whip. Now, the preparatory movement and stroke depart from the curve and approximate the straight line, in proportion to the force of the gesture used. A suggestive gesture is usually made in easy, graceful curves, while in a strongly emphatic gesture the arm is raised and sent forth much more directly. But

in any case the arm itself in almost any gesture is slightly curved. Rarely are the arm and hand so held as to make a straight line.

3. *A gesture either precedes or accompanies the vocal expression.* Suggestive and locative gestures precede the vocal expression. The psychology of gesture dictates this law. The idea of suggestion is in the mind. Gesture being a sign-language, the sign of the suggestion anticipates the vocal description, the eyes preceding the gesture, the gesture the spoken description. Since an emphatic gesture simply supplements the vocal emphasis, this gesture is given simultaneously with the vocal utterance. A violation of this principle by gesturing too soon or too late will demonstrate the incongruity. Learn to have the preparatory movement and the stroke well-timed.

Cautions. — Among the many faults in gesturing, the following are noted as things to be avoided : —

1. *Avoid gesture at the beginning or at the very close of a speech.* The reason for this admonition is obvious. Since gesture is largely a phase of emotional expression, one does not ordinarily reach the gesturing point in the introductory sentences; and to employ gestures then, usually indicates either mechanical movements or a lack of repose. And to employ gesture on the very closing words is to let the audience drop, as it were, without any warning. Further, gesture at this point obtrudes itself upon that direct contact of mind with mind, which should characterize the very close of an address.

2. *Avoid subjective gestures.* That is, gesturing to yourself or toward yourself. Remember that any gesture that takes the attention of the audience from the thought either to the gesture or to the speaker, is a poor gesture, for it violates the first essential of public-speaking, — thought

communication. Hence many gestures often used by the dramatic reader are to be shunned; such as striking attitudes with hands clasped, or hand on the heart, or exhibiting your hands when you are speaking of some one's else hands, or pointing to any part of the body — in short, calling attention in any way to your person. True, a bit of impersonation may at times be called for, but rarely. There should be an exposition of the thought, not an exhibition of the speaker. It follows that gestures should curve out toward the audience, and not, as is sometimes done, in toward the speaker.

3. *Avoid see-saw gestures.* That is, beginning a gesture with one hand and then bringing in the other hand; or beginning with both hands, and then dropping one. It is true that good speakers occasionally do this, and at times, in suggestive gestures, it may be appropriate, but very rarely; for when an impulse to gesture is begun with one hand, or with both hands, that impulse will naturally work itself out along the lines originally intended. Gestures that are see-sawing — one hand up, then the other — show a lack of coördination, and are apt to appear studied.

4. *Avoid a too literal representation of figurative language.* It is amusing to note how some speakers will try to define the metes and bounds, the ins and outs of a figure of speech, instead of suggesting its broad outlines and leaving something to the imagination of the audience. For example, I have seen students, in speaking such sentences as, " Go back with me to the commencement of this century, and select what statesman you please," turn about and point backward, and in so doing make the further mistake of translating time as distance.

Duncan Campbell Lee, professor of oratory at Cornell University, relates the following as coming under his observation : A young man was declaiming a selection containing the following sentence : " A handful (*looking in his hand*) of men rushed up the incline (*motion of sending them up*). they were driven back again (*receding movement of hand*) and — where were they ? " (*looking in his hand again — ending with a " lost" look at the audience*).   Says Professor Hiram Corson : " Gesture results, or should result, from emotion, and should therefore be indefinite.   Mimetic gesture, or mimetic action of any kind, is rarely, if ever, in place."   He goes on to say that the meaning of such words as " rotatory " or " somersault " requires no illustration to an audience of ordinary intelligence ; and cites an example published in " Expression," where a popular public reader of Boston, in rendering the last two lines of Wordsworth's " Daffodils," —

> " And then my heart with pleasure fills,
>   And dances with the daffodils,"

put her hand to her heart and, with " pleasure," indicated by a sentimental flash of the eye upon the audience, danced a few graceful steps expressive of exuberant joy, and bowed herself off the platform amid the vociferous applause of the audience.   The reader's taste in this case was no worse than that of the audience that applauded her.   The incident shows how great the general lack of taste, and the need of systematic study of fitness in relation of thought to its expression.[1]

These imitative movements are affected by some elocutionists, and students adopt such gestures as the proper thing.   Avoid them.   They are rarely used in good interpretative reading, and certainly have no place in public speaking.

It may be added here, that since figures of speech are ordinarily used to illustrate the thought, the burden of the gesture expression should not be put upon such figures, but

---

[1] Corson: *The Voice and Spiritual Education*, p. 128.

rather reserved for emphasizing the thought itself,— the plain statements of the leading ideas.

5. *Avoid using too many gestures.* As in other elements of expression, too many gestures lose their force by monotony. You have seen speakers who were continually waving their arms and hands, producing a sort of windmill effect. Do not think that every idea must be painted on a banner and waved at the audience, or reflected in some way in the action. This is a mistake that many dramatic readers make,— every idea is pictured in some form upon the body. On this point Professor Corson says : —

I was once present, by accident, at a lecture given by a Delsarto-elocutionary woman, and in the course of the lecture, she presented what, she said, would be false gestures in reciting Whittier's "Maud Muller." She then recited the poem, with, according to her notions, true gestures, which were more in number than Cicero made, perhaps, in his orations against Catiline, or Demosthenes, in his "Oration on the Crown." Every idea of the poem told outwardly on her body.

If a woman, in reading "Maud Muller," has emotions which must find vent in gesture and various physical contortions, she ought to be put under treatment that would tone up her system.

A speaker with a nervous temperament, having an impulse to gesture frequently, needs to repress rather than encourage the use of gestures, and put the impulse on the vocal delivery. Avoid all side-twitchings and meaningless movements of the arms and hands, termed by the classic writers the "babbling of the hands"; but when a gesture is employed, make it strong and finished, realizing the purpose of its use in the execution. It is always best to reserve gestures for the strong places in a speech — they are then all the more forceful. Excess of action weakens, while economy of appropriate action strengthens.

Variety in gesture is desirable. The direct, emphatic gesture is the preferable type for the public speaker, but do not be confined to a single gesture for this single type. Speaking on this subject, the Rev. Herrick Johnson, of Chicago, himself widely known as a forcible speaker, says : —

Economy of gesture is just like precision in speech. You do not want too many words to express thought, but you want enough. Not two arms where one would suffice. Not a gesture for every varying thought, and not too frequent gestures for the same thought. For example, the digital finger is very strong in gesture if used with economy. If it is used now and then you can send the thought right down into the hearer's heart by shaking your forefinger at him. But if you are shaking it all the time, what does it amount to?

6. *Do not gesture without an impulse to gesture.* This is, after all, the conclusion of the whole matter. To be sure, in the process of training, directions previously given may well be followed for the sake of practice ; for as the physical reacts upon the mental, a given physical movement may induce a corresponding emotion. But in the actual process of delivery the rule as laid down should be scrupulously followed. Attempting to put on gesture from the outside has been so glaringly the fault of elocutionists as to offend people of culture, and prejudice them against any attempts at teaching the art of public utterance. In the synthesis of delivery, if the mind and emotions are active, and are freeing themselves through an active and well-poised physical medium, appropriate gestures will make themselves. At any rate, conscious attention to gestures, as such, should be reduced to a minimum. Those that come spontaneously are the best, and enough. Even in the preliminary training of a school or college, a disproportionate amount of time is often given to the subject of gesture ; the control, poise, and grace

that characterize a finished speaker usually come after much practice in public speaking.

SUMMARY.

Action, which includes physical earnestness and gesture, is an important means of expression. It manifests itself especially in the speaker's carriage and in the movements of his arms and hands. The speaker should sometimes stimulate, and should always control and guide, the impulse to actional expression; but he should never gesture without such impulse.

2 minute talk,

CHAPTER XII.

GENERAL SUGGESTIONS.

Style of Delivery. — In the opening chapter it was shown that the basis of the best speaking lies in the best conversation; that the act of speaking is only the enlarged conversation that comes from speaking to a collection of individuals; that the most effective public speaking comes from *talking* to the audience. Now, if the student can from the outset be persuaded to take this attitude toward any audience he may address, he has gained more than he could from a year's study and practice of the technique of delivery. This conversational basis in speech is of the very essence of the problem. If the audience is to be impressed by your thoughts, convinced of your convictions, and persuaded of your beliefs, its attention should not be distracted by a method of communication outside the ordinary experience. And if here and there a speaker who has special qualities of force or attractiveness attains a certain measure of success by another method, it does not affect the truth of this underlying principle.

Then, too, the conversational style of delivery accords with modern taste; for oratory, like other arts, may have a certain type or style, varying with changing conditions. The style of popular oratory has undergone a marked change in this country — from the heavy and bombastic to the simple and direct — within the past twenty-five years. It was Wendell Phillips who more than any other one

man first set the fashion which has largely done away
with barn-storming and haranguing.   Curtis, in the excerpt
quoted on p. 100, describes his manner as that of a "gentleman conversing."   Says Colonel Thomas Wentworth
Higginson : —

The keynote to the oratory of Wendell Phillips lay in this : that
it was essentially conversational — the conversational raised to the
highest power.   Perhaps no orator ever spoke with so little apparent effort, or began so entirely on the plane of his average hearers.
It was as if he simply repeated, in a little louder tone, what he had
just been saying to some familiar friend at his elbow.   The collo-
quialism was never relaxed, but it was familiarity without loss of
dignity.   Then, as the argument went on, the voice grew deeper,
the action more animated, and the sentences came in a long,
sonorous swell, still easy and graceful, but powerful as the soft
stretch of a tiger's paw.

The conversational style is first of all *spontaneous*.   The
speaker's individuality speaks along with his words; he is
what we call "natural."   It is so easy and tempting for
the young speaker to imitate some one whose delivery he
particularly admires, forgetting that had the model sunk *his*
individuality by copying another he would not have seemed
so admirable.   Secondly, the conversational style is simple
and *direct*.   There are no superfluous frills and flourishes in
getting the message from the speaker directly to the audience.   The speaker's art is not that of the dancer, as is so
often thought.   It is rather that of the wrestler.   There must
be a personal grapple with the audience.   The speaker's
aim must be not to have the audience admire him, but
to have it follow him.   Lastly, the conversational style is
characterized by *variety*.   This comes from the speaker's
spontaneity and from a flexibility of voice and body that
produce frequent and natural changes.

As was shown in Chapter III, this conversational style, or what has been referred to as the conversational *basis*, does not mean that one is to speak in a large room to a number of persons in the same manner as he would speak to a single person standing by his side. If he did he would not be heard; or, if heard, his words might fall flat and lifeless. Colonel Higginson, in the quotation given above, shows that Mr. Phillips did not so speak. Public speaking is a magnified, heightened conversation. It is, as Colonel Higginson says, "the conversational *raised to its highest power !*" Oratory in its higher reaches, where the emotional element predominates over the mental, is characterized by an idealized language which lifts speakers and hearers above the humdrum of common speech. It must be admitted, too, that something depends upon the character of the audience. By an audience of average culture nowadays — and beware of talking *down* to any audience — the simplicity of conversation is relished, as of one man talking earnestly with another, resting down upon his subject and making that speak. Mere emotionalism tends to disappear with the advance of civilization, but certain classes of men, such as judges in courts of law and college professors, used to hearing much speaking and trained to value the intellectual, are perhaps inclined to undervalue, as young speakers are inclined to overvalue, the emotional element, for the purposes of popular oratory. It was noticed, for example, that Mr. Bryan's style of delivery when speaking to a university audience was more quiet than when giving practically the same speech the next afternoon at a political barbecue. Mr. Sheppard, in his *Before an Audience*, remarks that even Phillips "required listeners that were accustomed to listening." And yet, after making all allowances for varying conditions, the best public speaking is fundamentally strong, direct *talk*.

Stage-fright. — It is quite impossible to diagnose that common malady known as stage-fright. Usually it afflicts the speaker during the first few seconds, or first few minutes, of his speech. Most speakers have it, in varying degrees. Preachers tell us, for example, that even after long experience, they never begin their weekly sermons without the most intense nervousness. True, experiences vary. Gladstone, when asked if he never became nervous before speaking, said that he often did in opening a debate, but never in replying.

An amusing feature of this matter is, that young speakers are apt to think that they are the only ones that become seriously embarrassed. And right here is the lesson : trained speakers learn to control their embarrassment. It should be remembered that a nervous tension, if brought under control, may prove a help rather than a hindrance to the speaker, for it puts a nerve-force into his delivery that might otherwise be wanting. How attain that control ? There is no way but through practice in speaking to audiences. Continued practice, if it does not eliminate all embarrassment, gradually does reduce the earlier terrors. The practice should, of course, be directed along right lines. Nervousness may be aided much by a feeling of mental and physical preparedness. Have the speech thoroughly in hand long enough beforehand to give both mind and body a rest. Students often make the mistake of worrying over a speech up to the very moment of its delivery. This method is suicidal. Even speakers of experience sometimes fail to realize how much the success or failure of a speech depends upon physical conditions. To undergo the severe nervous strain of public speaking, mind and body should be fresh. The day preceding an athletic event the trained contestant either rests or exercises very moderately. So, if a speech is to be given at night, say, the speaker should wholly lay it aside during the afternoon and go for a walk or go to sleep — do anything but exhaust faculties that will be needed in the evening.

Control is also effected through the communicative, conversational attitude, as one rises to speak, and by an exercise of the will. Again, self-confidence should be cultivated. Self-fear is quite as often a cause of stage-fright as is a fear of the audience. Encourage a feeling that you and your audience are getting on well together. Self-confidence is not undue conceit, or "brag, brass, and bluster"; it is having the courage of one's convictions. It is that self-reliance which enables one to rise to the occasion. It is that confidence which leads the speaker to say to himself, "I know what I want to say and I am able to say it."

Study and Practice. — Like every other art, public speaking demands long-continued study and practice. The most proficient always feel there is room for improvement; and like other things in life, if one is earnestly striving to reach an ideal, there is hope for him; if he thinks he has reached it, he is lost. The complex art of public address cannot be learned quickly, and should never be taken up as a plaything. If you expect to be a speaker, make a business of the study, as you would of anything else worth learning. Do not dabble in it. A little dabbling with the technique given in this book is useless. It is because we have so many dabblers that we have so many bunglers. And by way of repetition, — do not expect to correct in a month a fault that is the habit of years.

Along with practice in vocal technique, the student should daily practise *reading aloud*, — preferably to a listener or listeners. And even after vocal technique may have been fairly well mastered, daily practice in oral reading should be continued, for in intelligent and sympathic reading aloud may be found a powerful means of culture. The scarcity of good readers is another reason for the acquisition of the art. Ask the average college graduate to read a piece of simple prose, and hear him jumble it! Says Professor Edward Dowden, in his *New Studies in Literature :* —

The reading which we should desire to cultivate is intelligent reading, that is, it should express the meaning of each passage clearly; sympathetic reading, that is, it should convey the feeling delicately; musical reading, that is, it should move in accord with the melody and harmony of what is read, be it in verse or prose.

To attain this, the reader must train the eye to look ahead of the vocalization and take in a clause or a sentence at a glance; that is, it should be phrase-reading, not word-reading. In reading in public, directness should be cultivated by allowing the eyes to play back and forth from the book or manuscript to the audience. At the beginning of a given sentence, the reader should be able to see through to the end of that sentence, and the closing words should be spoken directly to the audience, independently of the book, then return again to the copy. This power can be acquired by practice.

Practice, indeed, is the main thing. Certain incurable defects may be fatal, certain natural qualities are desirable, though not indispensable; the rest is work, — thorough preparation and continual practice. It is unfortunate if one must face an audience for the first time without previous training. The drill of school or college may be irksome, but the student should undertake it as he would any other task, — do it and make it count for something. If you have a declamation, an oration, or an argument to deliver, drill on the oral presentation. Speak to an imaginary audience. Invite your friends in and compel them to listen. Do not be afraid of drilling too much. I have heard students talk about getting "stale" who did not even enunciate clearly. An expert in technique to criticise and suggest is desirable, but not indispensable. Sometimes a friend who is not over-fastidious, has no dogmatic standards, and can judge of general effectiveness, is the most valuable sort of a critic. Take all the advice offered and — do not always act on it. A little experience will enable you to judge of its value; you will soon learn to know your leading faults yourself; and unless you are to surrender your individuality, you must be the final judge. And then, when the occasion arrives, put your technique in the background; let mental and moral earnestness be the predominant processes; and let the practice in technique unconsciously repeat itself in the final effort.

CONCLUSION.

Practice faithfully the technique of delivery until it becomes a second nature. Do not fail to make conscientious and thorough preparation for all those occasions, so frequent under the conditions of American life and government, when you will be called upon to speak: and thereby make general preparation for those times, unforeseen yet also frequent — those social or political crises in the affairs of a community, a State, or a Nation — when the public speaker, "sending the truth home," as Beecher defines oratory, "with all the resources of the living man," creates, moulds, and directs a public opinion that conduces to right thinking and right acting.

CHAPTER XIII.

SELECTIONS FOR PRACTICE.

THE ALAMO AND THE NEW SOUTH.

HENRY W. GRADY.

Extract from a speech delivered at the Dallas, Texas, State Fair,
October 26, 1887.

MEN, and especially young men, look back for their inspiration to what is best in their traditions. Thermopylæ cast Spartan sentiments in heroic mould, and sustained Spartan arms for more than a century. Thermopylæ had survivors to tell the story of its defeat. The Alamo had none. Though voiceless, it shall speak from its dumb walls. Liberty cried to Texas as God called from the clouds unto Moses. Bowie and Fannin, though dead, still live. Their voices rang above the din of Goliad and the glory of San Jacinto, and they marched with the Texas veterans who rejoiced at the birth of Texas independence. It is the spirit of the Alamo that moved above the Texas soldiers as they charged like demigods through a thousand battle-fields, and it is the spirit of the Alamo that whispers from their graves and ennobles the soil that was crimsoned with their blood.

In the spirit of this inspiration and in the thrill of the amazing growth that surrounds you, my young friends, it will be strange if the young men of Texas do not carry the

Lone Star into the heart of the struggle. The South needs her sons to-day more than when she summoned them to the forum to maintain her political supremacy, more than when the bugle called them to the field to defend issues put to the arbitrament of the sword. It is ours to show that as she prospered with slaves she shall prosper still more with freemen; ours to see that from the lists she entered in poverty she shall emerge in prosperity; ours to carry the transcending traditions of the old South, from which none of us can in honor or in reverence depart, unstained and unbroken into the new. Let every man here pledge himself, in this high and ardent hour, that in death and earnest loyalty, in patient painstaking and care, he shall watch her interest, advance her fortune, defend her fame, and guard her honor as long as life shall last.

With such consecrated service, what could we not accomplish; what riches we should gather for her; what glory and prosperity we should render to the Union; what blessings we should gather unto the universal harvest of humanity! As I think of it, a vision of surpassing beauty unfolds to my eyes. I see a South, the home of fifty millions of people, who rise up every day to call from blessed cities, vast hives of industry and of thrift; her country-sides the treasures from which their resources are drawn; her streams vocal with whirring spindles; her valleys tranquil in the white and gold of the harvest; her mountains showering down the music of bells, as her slow-moving flocks and herds go forth from their folds; her rulers honest and her people loving, and her homes happy and their hearthstones bright, and their waters still and their pastures green; her wealth diffused and poorhouses empty, her churches earnest

and all creeds lost in the gospel.   Peace and sobriety walking hand in hand through her borders ; honor in her homes ;
uprightness in her midst; plenty in her fields; straight and
simple faith in the hearts of her sons and daughters; her
two races walking together in peace and contentment.

All this, my country, and more can we do for you.   As I
look the vision grows, the splendor deepens, the horizon
falls back, the skies open their everlasting gates, and the
glory of the Almighty God streams through as He looks
down on His people who have given themselves unto Him
and leads them from one triumph to another until they have
reached a glory unspeaking, and the whirling stars, as in
their courses through Arcturus they run to the milky way,
shall not look down on a better people or happier land.

THE AMERICAN UNIVERSITY AND AMERICAN CITIZENSHIP.

WOODROW WILSON.

*From his address delivered on the occasion of his inauguration as
President of Princeton University, October 25, 1902.*

American universities serve a free nation, whose progress,
whose power, whose prosperity, whose happiness, whose integrity depend upon individual initiative and the sound
sense and equipment of the rank and file.   Their history,
moreover, has set them apart to a character and service of
their own.   They are not mere seminaries of scholars.   They
never can be.   Most of them, the greatest of them and the
most distinguished, were first of all great colleges before
they became universities, and their task is twofold, — the

production of a great body of informed and thoughtful men, and the production of a small body of trained scholars and investigators. It is one of their functions to take large bodies of young men up to the places of outlook whence the world of thought and affairs is to be viewed; it is another of their functions to take some men, a little more mature, a little more studious, men self-selected by aptitude and industry, into the quiet libraries and laboratories where the close contacts of study are learned which yield the world new insight into the processes of nature, of reason, and of the human spirit. These two functions are not to be performed separately, but side by side, and are to be informed with one spirit, the spirit of enlightenment, a spirit of learning which is neither superficial nor pedantic, which values life more than it values the mere acquisitions of the mind.

There are other things besides mere material success with which we must supply our generation. It must be supplied with men who care more for principles than for money, for the right adjustments of life than for the gross accumulations of profit. The problems that call for sober thoughtfulness and mere devotion are as pressing as those which call for practical efficiency. We are here not merely to release the faculties of men for their own use, but also to quicken their social understanding, instruct their consciences, and give them the catholic vision of those who know their just relations to their fellow-men. Here in America, for every man touched with nobility, for every man touched with the spirit of our institutions, social service is the high law of duty, and every American university must square its standards by that law or lack its national title. It is serving the nation to give men the enlightenments of a general training; it is serving the nation to equip fit men for thorough scientific investigation and for the tasks of exact scholarship, for science and scholarship carry the truth forward from generation to generation and give the certain touch of knowledge to the processes of life. But the whole service demanded is not rendered until something is added to the mere training of the undergraduate and the mere equipment of the investigator, something ideal and of the very spirit of all action. The final synthesis of learning is in philosophy. You shall most clearly judge the spirit of a university if you judge by the philosophy it teaches; and the philosophy of conduct is what every wise man should wish to derive from his knowledge of the thoughts and the affairs of the generations that have gone before him. We are not put into this world to sit still and know; we are put into it to act.

I have said already, let me say again, that in such a place as this we have charge, not of men's fortunes, but of their spirits. This is not the place in which to teach men their specific tasks, except their tasks be those of scholarship and investigation; it is the place in which to teach them the relations which all tasks bear to the work of the world. Some men there are who are condemned to learn only the technical skill by which they are to live; but these are not the men whose privilege it is to come to a university. University men ought to hold themselves bound to walk the upper roads of usefulness which run along the ridges and command views of the general fields of life. This is why I believe general training, with no particular occupation in view, to be the very heart and essence of university training, and the indispensable foundation of every special development of knowledge or of aptitude that is to lift a man to his profession or a scholar to his function of investigation.

A new age is before us, in which, it would seem, we must lead the world. No doubt we shall set it an example unprecedented, not only in the magnitude and telling perfection of our industries and arts, but also in the splendid scale and studied detail of our university establishments; the spirit of the age will lift us to every great enterprise. But the ancient spirit of sound learning will also rule us; we shall demonstrate in our lecture rooms again and again, with increasing volume of proof, the old principles that have made us free and great; reading men shall read here the chastened thoughts that have kept us young and shall make us pure; the school of learning shall be the school of memory and of ideal hope; and the men who spring from our loins shall take their lineage from the founders of the republic.

CHRISTIAN CITIZENSHIP.

CHARLES H. PARKHURST.

The fundamental service which the church has to render in the line of municipal or national betterment is to develop in Christians as such a civic consciousness. To an American the Stars and Stripes ought to be as actually a part of his religion as the Sermon on the Mount. Other things being equal, it is as urgently the obligation of a Christian to go to the polls on election day as it is for him to go to the Lord's table on communion day.

That sense of the holy obligation which citizenship involves must be made part of our Christian religion. It must be taught from the pulpit, rehearsed in the home, re-iterated in the Sunday-school, and practised in the life. I wish the time might come when we could have our national colors displayed in the sanctuary; not simply hung from the belfry in a shy kind of way on the Fourth of July and the twenty-second of February, but made a permanent part of sanctuary decoration.

The old Hebrew never thought of patriotism as anything but a constituent part of religion. To him it was religion in its political aspects. I wish there were some way in which we could make civic virtue part of our creed. It would be a tremendous gain if we could all of us come to conceive of, and to handle, civic duties, such as attending the primaries and going to the polls, as lying on religious ground and contained within Christian jurisdiction.

The instant effect of such civic consciousness would be to bring the citizen into direct practical relations to his city or country, and to make him feel in regard to his city, for example, "This is my city." No matter how many mayors or aldermen or police captains you have, it is your city all the same, and no city is safe unless its citizens tread steadily on the heels of those who have been hired to do the town's business. The mayor is bound to look after the citizens, but the citizens are just as much bound to look after the mayor. The police must watch the people, but the people must watch the police.

The evil will have to be overcome with the good, and personality is the thing that will have to do it. It will have to be done by men with convictions and with the courage of their convictions. It will have to be done by men who remember always that the security and the honor of the community lies not so much in its greatest statesmen, in its powerful leaders, or even in its educational advantages, as it does in the number of its men with whom righteousness is a chronic passion, civic duty a part of Christianity.

SOURCES OF OUR NATIONAL STRENGTH.

WHITELAW REID.

Extract from an address delivered in Carnegie Hall, Pittsburg, Pennsylvania, November 6, 1902.

We as Americans are intolerant believers in our form of government. Every child learns to think that it is the best in the world, not only for us but for all men. Every demagogue learns to bellow forth his unlimited, unquestioning certainty of that superiority and universal applicability. I am not here to dispute the belief — only to define the facts about it. If our form of government is the best, it cannot be so because it is the cheapest. On the contrary, it is one of the most expensive in the world. Nor can it be the best because it is the most efficient. On the contrary, it is one of the slowest in the world; the most complicated, cumbrous, and limited. And even within the spheres in which it will work, our form of government is not the easiest to work. On the contrary, it requires, to keep it running successfully, more public spirit, more study about candidates, more time for multitudinous elections, more watchfulness of public officials, and a higher average of intelligence than any other in the world. Now, if these things are so, if our government does in any measure have these defects, then the old question of the Philistines comes up with insistent force, " Wherein lies its great strength ? "

The answer has become a truism. Its strength lies in the quality of man it develops. The real merit is not in the machinery, but in the skilled intelligence absolutely required to frame and to work it; in the combination of respect for authority on the one hand, with training in individual initiative on the other, which this work brings out and which the government has thus far scrupulously and religiously guarded.

We brought the respect for authority from the birthplace of the common law; and in proportion as harshness from its officers was resented in the old home, in like proportion the law itself was instinctively elevated into a veritable pillar of cloud by day and of fire by night in the wilderness of the New World. We found the individual initiative in the necessities of an untamed continent; were driven to it, shut up to it at every turn, — in the imperative beginning of orderly self-government at a thousand isolated spots, — in the long-protracted struggle with wild lands, wild beasts, and wild men, — till it became the inheritance of the race; till under its stimulus men found their solitary way through trackless woods to make lonely clearings or start frontier settlements across the Alleghanies, through trackless prairies to possess the Mississippi Valley, through alkali deserts to wrest their gold from the mountains, and at last through the Sierras to scatter up and down the enchanted shore of the Pacific. To such a continental conquest of nature and of men have those two traits of the fathers brought us: their respect for authority and their widest freedom of individual initiative. These, with the original vigor of the stock, have made Americans what they are; and by consequence have made this blessed country of ours the joy and pride and hope of our lives. To harm either is criminal — whether to break down respect for authority by unlawful combinations, tricky evasions, and open defiance of order, or to cramp the widest freedom of the individual in any lawful enterprise or labor anywhere. Whoever or what-ever now dares to interfere with the permanent union of these two traits and their continued development in the American life, is an enemy to the Republic — whether known as political boss, or as trust, or as trade union.

This is the line along which the future of the Republic may be safeguarded. It is to endure, if at all, because the latest generations hold fast to the faith and practice of the fathers, respect for authority, and the widest liberty for individual activities. Mr. Dalzell once quoted to you very aptly the illuminating definition of civilization, given by a philosophic Frenchman. It is, said M. Guizot, the progress of society and the progress of the individual. But the society cannot make progress without that respect for authority which is its corner-stone; and the individual can-not make progress without that freedom of initiative which is the essence of liberty itself.

If society makes progress, and the individual does not, you have the condition, not of the Republic, which, we fondly trust, is to endure forever, but of the despotism which we have hoped was passing away. Let us not lose our heads in the midst of our bewildering prosperity, and risk shipwreck by getting out of sight of the old landmarks. We are the oldest republic in the world (save those so small as to be negligible), but our years do not yet cover the span the Psalmist assigned to two human lives, while those of the monarchies and despotisms count by thousands. Other republics, long since passed away, have lasted as long as we, and borne for their time as great a sway in the world. Be not deceived. Strong as this Republic is, it is not strong enough — let us hope it will never be unjust enough — to let either labor shut any of its children out of learning a trade or capital shut any of them out of going into trade. You cannot preserve the triumphant democracy and insure the American future unless you preserve the American citizen in his habit as he was, revering the law, respecting authority, and beyond that, still limited in his free activities by no master below God.

THE PHILIPPINE QUESTION.

ALBERT J. BEVERIDGE.

From a speech delivered in the United States Senate, January 9, 1900.

The question of our policy toward the Philippine Islands is deeper than any question of party politics; deeper than any question of the isolated policy of our country even; deeper even than any question of constitutional power. It is elemental. It is racial. God has not been preparing the English-speaking and Teutonic peoples for a thousand years for nothing but vain and idle self-contemplation and self-admiration. No! He has made us the master organizers of the world to establish system where chaos reigns. He has given us the spirit of progress to overwhelm the forces of reaction throughout the earth. He has made us adepts in government that we may administer government among savage and senile peoples. Were it not for such a force as this, the world would relapse into barbarism and might. And of all our race He has marked the American people as His chosen nation to finally lead in the regeneration of the world. This is the divine mission of America, and it holds for us all the profit, all the glory, all the happiness, possible to man. We are trustees of the world's progress, guardians of its righteous peace. The judgment of the Master is upon us: " Ye have been faithful over a few things; I will make you ruler over many things."

What shall history say of us? Shall it say that we renounced that holy trust, left the savage to his base condition, the wilderness to the reign of waste, deserted duty, abandoned glory, forgot our sordid profit even, because we feared our strength, and read the charter of our powers with the doubter's eye and the quibbler's mind? Shall it say that, called by events to captain and command the proudest, ablest, purest race of history in history's noblest work, we declined that great commission? Our fathers would not have had it so. No! They founded no paralytic government incapable of the simplest acts of administration. They planted no sluggard people, passive while the world's work calls them. They established no reactionary nation. They unfurled no retreating flag.

That flag has never paused in its onward march. Who dares halt it now — now, when history's largest events are carrying it forward; now, when we are at last one people, strong enough for any task, great enough for any glory destiny can bestow? How comes it that our first century closes with the process of consolidating the American people into a unit just accomplished, and quick upon the stroke of that great hour presses upon us our world opportunity, world duty, and world glory, which none but a people welded into an indivisible nation can achieve or perform?

Blind indeed is he who sees not the hand of God in events so vast, so harmonious, so benign. Reactionary indeed is the mind that perceives not that this vital people is the strongest of the saving forces of the world; that our place, therefore, is at the head of the constructing and redeeming nations of the earth; and that to stand aside while events march on is a surrender of our interests, a betrayal of our duty as blind as it is base. Craven indeed is the heart that fears to perform a work so golden and so noble; that dares not win a glory so immortal.

Do you tell me that it will cost us money? When did America ever measure duty by financial standards? Do you tell me of the tremendous toil required to overcome the vast difficulties of our task? What mighty work for the world, for humanity, even for ourselves, has ever been done with ease? Even our bread must we eat by the sweat of our faces. Why are we charged with power such as no people ever knew of if we are not to use it in a work such as no people ever wrought? We will dispute the divine meaning of the fable of the talents.

Do you remind me of the precious blood that must be shed, the lives that must be given, the broken hearts of loved ones for their slain? And this is indeed a heavier price than all combined. And yet as a nation every historic duty we have done, every achievement we have accomplished, has been by the sacrifice of our noblest sons. Every holy memory that glorifies the flag is of those heroes who died that its onward march might not be stayed. It is the nation's dearest lives yielded for the flag that makes it dear to us; it is the nation's most precious blood poured out for it that makes it precious to us. That flag is woven of heroism and grief, of the bravery of men, and women's tears, of righteousness and battle, of sacrifice and anguish, of triumph and glory. It is these which make our flag a holy thing. Who would tear from that sacred banner the glorious legends of a single battle where it has waved on land or sea? What son of a soldier of the flag whose father fell beneath it on any field would surrender that proud record for the heraldry of a king? In the cause of civilization, in the service of the Republic anywhere on earth, Americans consider wounds the noblest decorations man can win, and count the giving of their lives a glad and precious duty.

Pray God that spirit never fails. Pray God time may never come when Mammon and the love of ease shall so debase our blood that we will fear to shed it for the flag and its imperial destiny. Pray God the time may never come when American heroism is but a legend like the story of the Cid, American faith in our mission and our might a dream dissolved, and the glory of our mighty race departed.

And that time will never come. We will renew our youth at the fountain of new and glorious deeds. We will exalt our reverence for the flag by carrying it to a noble future as well as by remembering its ineffable past. Its immortality will not pass, because everywhere and always we will acknowledge and discharge the solemn responsibilities our sacred flag, in its deepest meaning, puts upon us. And so, with reverent hearts, where dwells the fear of God, the American people move forward to the future of their hope and the doing of His work.

OUR POLICY TOWARD THE PHILIPPINES.

GEORGE F. HOAR.

From a speech delivered in the United States Senate, May 22, 1900.

A famous orator once imagined the nations of the world uniting to erect a column to Jurisprudence in some stately capital. Each country was to bring the name of its great jurist to be inscribed on the side of the column, with a sentence stating what he and his country through him had done toward establishing the reign of law in justice for the benefit of mankind.

Rome said, "Here is Numa, who received the science of law from the nymph Egeria in the cavern and taught its message to his countrymen. Here is Justinian, who first reduced law to a code, made its precepts plain, so that all mankind could read it, and laid down the rules which should govern the dealing of man with man in every transaction of life."

France said, "Here is D'Aguesseau, the great chancellor, to whose judgment-seat pilgrims from afar were wont to repair to do him reverence."

England said, "Here is Erskine, who made it safe for men to print the truth, no matter what tyrant might dislike to read it."

Virginia said, "Here is Marshall, who breathed the vital principle into the Constitution, infused into it, instead of the letter that killeth, the spirit that maketh alive, and enabled it to keep state and nation each in its appointed bounds, as the stars abide in their courses."

I have sometimes fancied that we might erect here in the

capital of the country a column to American Liberty which alone might rival in height the beautiful and simple shaft which we have erected to the fame of the Father of the Country. I can fancy each generation bringing its inscription, which should recite its own contribution to the great structure of which the column should be but the symbol.

The generation of the Puritan and the Pilgrim and the Huguenot claims the place of honor at the base : "I brought the torch of freedom across the sea. I cleared the forest. I subdued the savage and the wild beast. I laid in Christian liberty and law the foundations of empire."

The next generation says: "What my fathers founded I builded. I left the seashore to penetrate the wilderness. I planted schools and colleges and courts and churches."

Then comes the generation of the great colonial day : "I stood by the side of England on many a hard-fought field. I helped humble the power of France. I saw the lilies go down before the lion at Louisburg and Quebec. I carried the cross of St. George in triumph in Martinique and the Havana. I knew the stormy pathways of the ocean. I followed the whale from the Arctic to the Antarctic seas, among tumbling mountains of ice and under equinoctial heat, as the great English orator said, 'No sea not vexed by my fisheries; no climate not witness to my toils.' "

Then comes the generation of the Revolutionary time : "I encountered the power of England. I declared and won the independence of my country. I placed that declaration on the eternal principles of justice and righteousness which all mankind have read, and on which all mankind will one day stand. I affirmed the dignity of human nature and the right of the people to govern themselves. I devised the securities against popular haste and delusion which made that right secure. I created the Supreme Court and the Senate. For the first time in history I made the right of the people to govern themselves safe, and established institutions for that end which will endure forever."

The next generation says : " I encountered England again. I vindicated the right of an American ship to sail the seas the wide world over without molestation. I made the American sailor as safe at the ends of the earth as my fathers had made the American farmer safe in his home. I proclaimed the Monroe doctrine in the face of the Holy Alliance, under which sixteen republics have joined the family of nations. I filled the Western Hemisphere with republics from the Lakes to Cape Horn, each controlling its own destiny in safety and in honor."

Then comes the next generation: "I did the mighty deeds which in your younger years you saw and which your fathers told. I saved the Union. I put down the rebellion. I freed the slave. I made of every slave a free-man, and of every freeman a citizen, and of every citizen a voter."

Then comes another who did the great work in peace, in which so many of you had an honorable share : "I kept the faith. I paid the debt. I brought in conciliation and peace instead of war. I secured in the practice of nations the great doctrine of expatriation. I devised the homestead system. I covered the prairie and the plain with happy homes and with mighty states. I crossed the continent and joined together the seas with my great railroads. I declared the manufacturing independence of America, as my fathers affirmed its political independence. I built up our vast domestic commerce. I made my country the richest, freest, strongest, happiest people on the face of the earth."

And now what have we to say ? What have we to say ? Are we to have a place in that honorable company ? Must we engrave on that column : " We repealed the Declaration of Independence. We changed the Monroe doctrine from a doctrine of eternal righteousness and justice, resting on the consent of the governed, to a doctrine of brutal selfishness, looking only to our own advantage. We crushed the only republic in Asia. We made war on the only Christian people in the East. We converted a war of glory to a war of shame. We vulgarized the American flag. We introduced perfidy into the practice of war. We inflicted torture on unarmed men to extort confession. We put children to death. We established reconcentrado camps. We devasted provinces. We baffled the aspirations of a people for liberty."

No. Never ! Never ! Other and better counsels will yet prevail. The hours are long in the life of a great people. The irrevocable step is not yet taken.

Let us at least have this to say : We too have kept the faith of the fathers. We took Cuba by the hand. We delivered her from her age-long bondage. We welcomed her to the family of nations. We set mankind an example never beheld before of moderation in victory. We led hesitating and halting Europe to the deliverance of their beleaguered ambassadors in China. We marched through a hostile country — a country cruel and barbarous — without anger or revenge. We returned benefit for injury and pity for cruelty. We made the name of America beloved in the East as in the West. We kept faith with the Philippine people. We kept faith with our own history. We kept our national honor unsullied. The flag which we received without a rent we handed down without a stain.

AMERICA A WORLD REPUBLIC.

ALBERT J. BEVERIDGE.

Extract from his speech opening the Republican campaign, delivered in the Auditorium at Chicago, September 25, 1900.

" Westward the Star of Empire takes its Way." Not the star of kingly power, for kingdoms are everywhere dissolving in the increasing rights of men; not the star of autocratic oppression, for civilization is brightening and the liberties of the people are broadening under every flag that floats. But the star of empire, as Washington used the word when he called this Republic an "empire"; as Jefferson understood it when he declared our form of government ideal for extending "our empire"; as Marshall understood it, when he closed a noble period of an immortal constitutional opinion by naming the domain of the American people "our empire." This is the "empire" of which the prophetic voice declared " Westward the Star of Empire takes its Way " — the star of the empire of liberty and law, of commerce and communication, of social order and the Gospel of our Lord — the star of the empire of the civilization of the world. Westward *that* star of empire takes its course. And to-day it illumines our path of duty across the Pacific into the islands and lands where Providence has called us.   In that path the American government is marching forward, opposed at every step by those who deny the right of the Republic to plant the institutions of the flag where events have planted that flag itself.

Fellow-Americans, this is no partisan conflict.   It is no unprecedented struggle.   It is the ever old and yet the ever new, because the ever elemental contest between the forces of growing nationality and those who resist it; between the forces of extending dominion and those who oppose it; between the forces that are making us the master people of the world and those who think that our activities should be confined to this continent forever.   It is the eternal duel between the forces of progress and reaction, of construction and disintegration, of growth and of decay.   The opponents of expansion are and always have been sincere.   But their sincerity did not make them right.   Their earnestness, ability, courage, could not give them victory.   They were struggling against the Fates.   They were resisting the onward forces which were making of the American people the master nation of the world — the forces that established us first as a separate politic body, then welded us into a national unit, indivisible; then extended our dominion from ocean to ocean over unexplored wildernesses; and now in the ripeness of time fling our authority and unfurl our flag almost all around the globe.   It is the " divine event" of American sovereignty among the governments of men for which these forces have been working since the Pilgrims landed on the red man's soil.   Men — patriotic, brave, and wise — have sought to stay that tremendous purpose of destiny, but their opposition was as the finger of a babe against the resistless pour of the Gulf Stream's mighty current.   For God's hand was in it all.   His plans were working out their glorious results.   And just as futile is resistance to the continuance to-day of the eternal movement of the American people toward the mastery of the world.

This is a destiny neither vague nor undesirable.   It is definite, splendid, and holy.   When nations shall war no more without the consent of the American Republic — what American heart thrills not with pride at that prospect? And yet our interests are weaving themselves so rapidly around the world that that time is almost here.   When governments stay the slaughter of human beings, because the American Republic demands it — what American heart thrills not with pride at that prospect?   And yet to-night there sits in Constantinople a sovereign who knows that that time is nearly here.   When the commerce of the world on which the world's peace hangs, travelling every ocean highway of earth, shall pass beneath the guns of the great Republic — what American heart thrills not at that prospect? Yet that time will be here before the second administration of the last American President of the nineteenth century and the first president of the twentieth century.   When any changing of the map of earth requires a conference of the powers, and when, at any congress of the nations, the American Republic will preside as the most powerful of powers and most righteous of judges — what American heart thrills not at that prospect?   And yet, that prospect is at hand, even as I speak.   It is the high and holy destiny of the American people, and from that destiny the American bugles will never sound retreat.   " Westward the Star of Empire takes its Way."

AMERICA AND INTERNATIONAL PEACE.

THEODORE ROOSEVELT.

Extract from a speech at the Lincoln Club Dinner, in New York City, February 13, 1899.

No sensible man will advocate our plunging rashly into a course of international knight-errantry; none will advocate our setting deliberately to work to build up a great colonial empire. But neither will any brave and patriotic man bid us shrink from doing our duty merely because this duty involves the certainty of strenuous effort and the possibility of danger. Some men of high reputation, from high motives, opposed the ratification of the treaty with Spain, just as they had previously opposed the war. The error was almost as great in one case as in the other and will be so adjudged by history. But back of the high motives of these men lay the two great impulses of sloth and fear; and well it was for us that the administration and the Senate disregarded them.

We should not lightly court danger and difficulty, but neither should we shirk from facing them, when in some way or other they must be met. We are a great nation and we are compelled, whether we will or not, to face the responsibilities that must be faced by all great nations. It is not in our power to avoid meeting them. All that we can decide is whether we shall meet them well or ill. There are social reformers who tell us that in the far distant future the necessity for fighting will be done away with, just as there are social reformers who tell us that in that long distant time the necessity for work — or, at least, for painful, laborious work — will be done away with. But just at present the nation, like the individual, which is going to do anything in the world must face the fact, that in order to do it, it must work and may have to fight. And it is only thus that great deeds can be done, and the highest and purest form of happiness acquired. Remember that peace itself, that peace after which all men crave, is merely the realization in the present of what has been bought by strenuous effort in the past. Peace represents stored-up effort of our fathers or of ourselves in the past. It is not a means — it is an end. You do not get peace by peace; you get peace as the result of effort. If you strive to get it by peace, you will lose it, that is all. If we ever grow to regard peace as a permanent condition; if we ever grow to feel that we can afford to let the keen, fearless, virile qualities of heart and mind and body be lost, then we will prepare the way for inevitable and shameful disaster in the future.

Peace is of true value only as we use it in part to make ready to face with untroubled heart, with fearless front, whatever the future may have in store for us. The peace which breeds timidity and sloth is a curse and not a blessing. The law of worthy national life, like the law of worthy individual life, is, after all, fundamentally, the law of strife. It may be strife military, it may be strife civic; but certain it is that only through strife, through labor, and painful effort, by grim energy and by resolute courage, we move on to better things.

A TALK ON BOOKS.

HENRY DRUMMOND.

Adapted from an address delivered in New York City, with a quotation added from Richard Le Gallienne.

To fall in love with a good book is to add a rich gift to life's experiences. It is to have a new influence pouring itself into our lives, a new teacher to inspire and refine us, a new friend to be by our side always, who, when life grows narrow and weary, will take us into his wider and calmer and higher world. Whether it be biography, introducing us to some humble life made great by duty done; or history, opening vistas into the movements and destinies of nations that have passed away; or poetry, making music of all the common things around us, and filling the fields, and the skies, and the work of the city and the cottage, with eternal meaning — whether it be these, or story-books, or religious books, or science, no one can become the friend of one good book without being made wiser and better.

I would not presume to recommend such a book to you. The beauty of a friend is that we discover him. And we must each taste the books that are accessible to us for ourselves. Do not be disheartened at first if you like none of them. That is possibly their fault, not yours. But search and search till you find what you like. In amazingly cheap form almost all the best books are now to be had; and I think every one owes it as a sacred duty to his mind to start a little library of his own. How much do we not do for our bodies? How much thought and money do they not cost us? And shall we not think a little, and pay a little, for *t*he clothing and adorning of the imperishable mind ? This private library may begin, perhaps, with a single volume, and grow at the rate of one or two a year ; but these, well chosen and well mastered, will become such a fountain of strength and wisdom that each shall be glad to add to his store.

A dozen books accumulated in this way may be better than a whole library. Do not be distressed if you do not like time-honored books, or classical works, or recommended books. Choose for yourself; plant yourself on your own instincts; that which is natural for us, that which nourishes us and gives us appetite, is that which is right for us. We have all different minds, and we are all at different stages of growth. Some other day we may find food in the recommended book, though we should possibly starve on it to-day. The mind develops and changes, and the favorites of this year may one day cease to interest us. Nothing better, indeed, can happen to us than to lose interest in a book we have often read; for it means that it has done its work upon us, and brought us up to its level, and taught us all it had to teach.

"Old Books to Read" — "Old Friends to Trust" — how can we estimate their value ?

"Books! those miraculous memories of high thoughts and golden moods; those silver shells, tremulous with the wonderful secrets of ocean life; those love-letters that pass from hand to hand of a thousand lovers that never meet; those honeycombs of dreams ; those orchards of knowledge; those still-beating hearts of the noble dead ; those mysterious signals that beckon along the darksome pathways of the past; voices through which the myriad whisperings of the earth

find perfect speech; oracles through which its mysteries call
like voices in moonlit woods; prisms of beauty; urns stored
with all the sweets of all the summers of time; immortal
nightingales that sing forever to the roses of life — Books!"

THE MASTERPIECE OF GOD.

ELBERT HUBBARD.

*Extract from an essay on Leonardo da Vinci in Volume X of
" Little Journeys," February, 1902.*

The human face is the masterpiece of God.

A woman's smile may have in it more sublimity than a
sunset; more pathos than a battle-scarred landscape; more
warmth than the sun's bright rays; more love than words
can say. The human face is the masterpiece of God.

The eyes reveal the soul, the mouth the flesh, the chin
stands for purpose, the nose means will. But over and behind all is that fleeting Something we call "expression."
This Something is not set or fixed; it is fluid as the ether,
changeful as the clouds that move in mysterious majesty
across the surface of a summer sky, subtle as the sob of
rustling leaves, — too faint at times for human ears, — elusive
as the ripples that play hide-and-seek over the bosom of a
placid lake.

And yet men have caught expression and held it captive.
On the walls of the Louvre hangs the "Mona Lisa" of
Leonardo da Vinci. This picture has been for four hundred
years an exasperation and an inspiration to every portrait-
painter who has put brush to palette. Well does Walter
Pater call it "The Despair of Painters." The artist was

over fifty years of age when he began the work, and he was four years in completing the task.

Completing, did I say? Leonardo's dying regret was that he had not completed this picture. And yet we might say of it, as Ruskin said of Turner's work, "By no conceivable stretch of the imagination can we say where this picture can be bettered or improved upon."

There is in the face all you can read into it and nothing more. It gives you what you bring and nothing else. It is as silent as the lips of Memnon, as voiceless as the Sphinx. It suggests to you every joy that you have ever felt, every sorrow you have ever known, every triumph you have ever experienced.

This woman is beautiful, just as all life is beautiful when we are in health. She has no quarrel with the world — she loves and she is loved again. No vain longing fills her heart, no feverish unrest disturbs her dreams, for her no crouching fears haunt the passing hours — that ineffable smile which plays around her mouth says plainly that life is good. And yet the circles about the eyes and the drooping lids hint of world-weariness and speak the message of Koheleth, and say, "Vanity of vanities, all is vanity."

"La Gioconda" is infinitely wise, for she has lived. That supreme poise is only possible to one who knows. All the experiences and emotions of manifold existence have etched and moulded that form and face until the body has become the perfect instrument of the soul.

Back of her stretches her life, a mysterious purple shadow. Do you not see the palaces turned to dust, the broken columns, the sunken treasures, the creeping mosses, and the rank ooze of fretted waters that have undermined cities and turned kingdoms into desert seas? The galleys of pagan Greece have swung wide for her on the unforgetting tide, for her soul dwelt in the body of Helen of Troy, and Pallas Athene has followed her ways and whispered to her even the secrets of the gods. Aye! not only was she Helen, but she was Leda, the mother of Helen. Then she was St. Anne, mother of Mary; and next she was Mary, visited by an angel in a dream, and followed by the wise men who had seen the Star in the East. The centuries, that are but thoughts, found her a Vestal Virgin in pagan Rome, when brutes were kings and lust stalked rampant through the streets. She was the bride of Christ and her fair frail body was flung to the wild beasts, and torn limb from limb while the multitude feasted on the sight.

True to the central impulse of her soul the Dark Ages rightly called her Cecilia, and then St. Cecilia, mother of sacred music, and later she ministered to men as Melania, the Nun of Tagaste; next as the daughter of William the Conqueror, the Sister of Charity who went through Italy, Spain, and France, and taught the women of the nunneries how to sew, to weave, to embroider, to illuminate books and make beauty, truth, and harmony manifest to human eyes. And so this Lady of the Beautiful Hands stood to Leonardo as the embodiment of a perpetual life; moving in a constantly ascending scale, gathering wisdom, graciousness, love, even as he himself in this life met every experience halfway and counted it joy, knowing that experience is the germ of power.

Life writes its history upon the face, so that all those who have had a like experience read and understand. The human face is the masterpiece of God.

PUBLIC OPINION AND AGITATION.

WENDELL PHILLIPS.

An extract from his lecture on " Public Opinion."

It is a singular fact that the freer a nation becomes, the more utterly democratic the form of its institutions, outside agitation — the pressure of public opinion to direct political action — becomes more and more necessary. In a country like ours, of absolute democratic equality, public opinion is not only omnipotent, it is omnipresent. There is no refuge from its tyranny; there is no hiding from its reach; and the result is that, if you take the old Greek lantern, and go about to seek among a hundred, you will find not one single American who really has not, or who does not fancy at least that he has, something to gain or lose in his ambition, his social life, or his business, from the good opinion and the votes of those about him. And the consequence is, that, — instead of being a mass of individuals, each one fearlessly blurting out his own convictions, — as a nation, compared with other nations, we are a mass of cowards. More than any other people, we are afraid of each other.

If you were a caucus to-night, Democratic or Republican, and I were your orator, none of you could get beyond the necessary and timid limitations of party. You not only would not demand, you would not allow me to utter, one word of what you really thought and what I thought. You would demand of me — and my value as a caucus speaker would depend entirely on the adroitness and the vigilance with which I met the demand — that I should not utter one single word which would compromise the vote of next week.

That is politics; so with the press. Seemingly independent, and sometimes really so, the press can afford only to mount the cresting wave, not go beyond it. The editor might as well shoot his reader with a bullet as with a new idea. He must hit the exact line of the opinion of the day.

This is the inevitable, the essential limitation of the press in a republican community. Our institutions, floating un-anchored on the shifting surface of popular opinion, cannot afford to hold back, or to draw forward, a hated question and compel a reluctant public to look at it and to consider it. Hence, as you see at once, the moment a large issue, twenty years ahead of its age, presents itself to the con-sideration of an empire or of a republic, just in proportion to the freedom of its institutions is the necessity of a plat-form outside of the press, of politics, and of its church whereon stand men with no candidate to elect, with no plan to carry, with no reputation to stake, with no object but the truth, no purpose but to tear the question open and let the light through it.

So much in explanation of a word infinitely hated, — agitation and agitators, — but an element which the progress of modern government has developed more and more every day. Republics exist only on the tenure of being constantly agitated. The republic which sinks to sleep, trusting to constitutions and machinery, to politicians and statesmen, for the safety of its liberties, never will have any. We must live like our Puritan fathers, who always went to church and sat down to dinner, when the Indians were in the neigh-borhood, with their musket-lock on the one side and a drawn sword on the other. No, there is no Canaan in politics. As health lies in labor, and there is no royal road to it but through toil, so there is no republican road to safety but in constant distrust. "In distrust," said Demosthenes, "are the nerves of the mind." Let us see to it that these sentinel nerves are ever on the alert. If the Alps, piled in cold and still sublimity, be the emblem of Despotism, the ever restless ocean is ours, which, girt within the eternal laws of gravitation, is pure only because never still.

THE TRIUMPH OF TRUTH.

THOMAS CARLYLE.

Adapted from "Past and Present."

In this — God's — world, with its wild, whirling eddies and mad, foam oceans, where men and nations perish as if without law, and judgment for an unjust thing is sternly delayed, dost thou think that there is therefore no justice? It is what the fool hath said in his heart. It is what the wise, in all times, were wise because they denied and knew forever not to be. I tell thee again, there is nothing else but justice. One strong thing I find here below: the just thing, the true thing.

My friend, if thou hadst all the artillery of Woolwich trundling at thy back in support of an unjust thing, and infinite bonfires visibly waiting ahead of thee to blaze centuries long for the victory on behalf of it, I would advise thee to call halt, to fling down thy baton, and say, "In Heaven's name, no!"

Thy "success"? Poor devil, what will thy success amount to? If the thing is unjust, thou hast not succeeded; no, not though bonfires blazed from north to south, and bells rang, and editors wrote leading articles, and the just things lay trampled out of sight, — to all mortal eyes an abolished and annihilated thing. . . .

For it is the right and noble alone that will have victory in this struggle; the rest is wholly an obstruction, a postponement, a fearful imperilment of the victory. Toward an eternal centre of right and nobleness, and of that only, is all confusion tending. We already know whither it is all tending; what will have victory, what will have none! The heaviest will reach the centre. The heaviest has its deflections; its obstructions; nay, at times its reboundings, its resiliences, whereupon some blockhead shall be heard jubilating, "See, your heaviest ascends!" but at all moments it is moving centreward, fast as is convenient for it; sinking, sinking; and, by laws older than the world, old as the Maker's first plan of the world, it has to arrive there.

Await the issue. In all battles, if you await the issue, each fighter has prospered according to his right. His right and his might, at the close of the account, were one and the same. He has fought with all his might, and in exact proportion to all his right he has prevailed. His very death is no victory over him. He dies indeed; but his work lives, very truly lives.

Fight on, thou brave, true heart; and falter not, through dark fortune and through bright. The cause thou fightest for, so far as it is true, no further, yet precisely so far, is very sure of victory. The falsehood alone of it will be conquered, will be abolished, as it ought to be; but the truth of it is part of Nature's own laws, coöperates with the world's eternal tendencies, and cannot be conquered.

CHARACTER ESSENTIAL FOR A GREAT LAWYER.

WENDELL PHILLIPS.

Selected from his lecture on " Idols."

It is a grave thing when a state puts a man among her jewels, the glitter of whose fame makes doubtful acts look heroic. The honors we grant mark how high we stand and they educate the future. The men we honor and the maxims we lay down in measuring our favorites show the level and morals of the time. A name has been in every one's mouth of late, and men have exhausted language in trying to express their admiration and respect. The courts have covered the grave of Mr. Choate with eulogy. Let us see what is their idea of a great lawyer. We are told that " he worked hard," "he never neglected his client," "he flung over the discussions of the forum the grace of a rare scholarship." "No pressure or emergency ever stirred him to an unkind word." A ripe scholar, a profound lawyer, a faithful servant to his client, a gentleman. This is a good record, surely. May he sleep in peace. What he earned God grant he may have. But the bar that seeks to claim for such a one a place among great jurists must itself be weak indeed. Not one high moral trait specified; not one patriotic act mentioned; not one patriotic service even claimed. Look at Mr. Webster's idea of what a lawyer should be in order to be called great, in the sketch he drew of Jeremiah Mason, and notice what stress he lays upon the religious and moral elevation and the glorious and high purposes which crown his life. Nothing of this now; nothing but incessant eulogy. But not a word of one effort to lift the yoke of cruel or unequal legislation from the neck of its victim; not one attempt to make the code of his country wiser, purer, better; not one effort to bless his times or breathe a higher moral purpose into the community.   Not one blow struck for right or for liberty, while the battle of the giants was going on about him; not one patriotic act to stir the hearts of his idolaters; not one public act of any kind whatever about whose merit friend or foe could even quarrel, unless when he scouted our great charter as a glittering generality, or jeered at the philanthropy which tried to practise the Sermon on the Mount.

When Cordus, the Roman senator, whom Tiberius murdered, was addressing his fellows, he began, "Fathers, they accuse me of illegal words; plain proof that there are no illegal deeds with which to charge me."   So with these eulogies.   Words, nothing but words; plain proof that there were no deeds to praise.   Yet this is the model which Massachusetts offers to the Pantheon of the great jurists of the world!

Suppose we stood in that lofty temple of jurisprudence, — on either side of us the statues of the great lawyers of every state and clime, — and let us see what part New England — Puritan, educated, free New England — would bear in the pageant.

Rome points to a colossal figure and says, "That is Papinian, who, when the Emperor Caracella murdered his own brother, and ordered the lawyer to defend the deed, went cheerfully to death, rather than sully his lips with the atrocious plea; and that is Ulpian, who, aiding his prince to put the army below the law, was massacred at the foot of a weak but virtuous throne."

And France stretches forth her grateful hands, crying, "That is D'Aguesseau, worthy, when he went to face an enraged king, of the farewell his wife addressed him, 'Go, forget that you have a wife and children to ruin, and remember only that you have France to save.'"

England says: "That is Coke, who flung the laurels of eighty years in the face of the first Stuart, in defence of the people. This is Selden, on every book of whose library you saw written the motto of which he lived worthy, 'Before everything, liberty!' That is Mansfield, silver tongued, who proclaimed, 'Slaves cannot breathe in England; if their lungs receive our air, that moment they are free.'"

Then New England shouts, "This is Choate, who made it safe to murder, and of whose health thieves asked before they began to steal!"

JURY ADDRESS.

DANIEL WEBSTER.

An extract from his speech in the White Murder Trial.

Gentlemen, this is a most extraordinary case. In some respects it has hardly a precedent anywhere, certainly none in our New England history. This bloody drama exhibited no suddenly excited, ungovernable rage. It was a cool, calculating, money-making murder. It was the weighing of money against life; the counting out of so many pieces of silver against so many ounces of blood.

An aged man, without an enemy in the world, in his own house and in his own bed, is made the victim of a butcherly murder for mere pay. Truly, here is a new

lesson for painters and poets. Whoever shall here-
after draw the portrait of murder, let him not give it the
grim visage of Moloch, — the brow knitted by revenge, the
face black with settled hate, and the bloodshot eye emitting
livid fires of malice. Let him draw rather a decorous,
smooth-faced, bloodless demon; a picture in repose rather
than in action; not so much an example of human nature
in its depravity and in its paroxyms of crime, as an infernal
being, a fiend, in the ordinary display and development of
his character.

The circumstances now clearly in evidence spread out
the whole scene before us. Deep sleep had fallen on the
destined victim and on all beneath his roof. A healthful old
man to whom sleep was sweet, the first sound slumbers of
the night held him in their soft but strong embrace. The
assassin enters, through the window already prepared, into
an unoccupied apartment. With noiseless foot he paces the
lonely hall half lighted by the moon. He winds up the
ascent of the stairs and reaches the door of the chamber.
He enters and beholds his victim before him. The face of the
innocent sleeper is turned from the murderer, and the beams
of the moon, resting on the gray locks of the aged temples,
show him where to strike. The fatal blow is given. Without a struggle or a motion the victim passes from the
repose of sleep to the repose of death. The murderer
retreats, retraces his steps to the window, passes out through
it as he came in, and escapes.

He has done the deed. No eye has seen him, no ear has
heard him, the secret is his own and it is safe. Ah!
Gentlemen, that was a dreadful mistake. Such a secret
can be safe nowhere. The whole creation of God has

neither nook nor corner where the guilty can bestow it and say it is safe. A thousand eyes turn at once to explore every man, every thing, every circumstance, connected with the time and place; a thousand ears catch every whisper; a thousand excited minds intensely dwell on the scene, shedding all their light, and ready to kindle the slightest circumstance into a blaze of discovery. Meantime the guilty soul cannot keep its own secret. It is false to itself; or, rather, it feels an irresistible impulse of conscience to be true to itself. It labors under its guilty possession and knows not what to do with it. The human heart was not made for the residence of such an inhabitant. The secret which the murderer possesses soon comes to possess him, and, like the evil spirits of which we read, it overcomes him and leads him whithersoever it will. He feels it beating at his heart, rising to his throat, and demanding disclosure. He thinks the whole world sees it in his face, reads it in his eyes, and almost hears its workings in the very silence of his thoughts. It has become his master. It betrays his discretion, it breaks down his courage, it conquers his prudence. When suspicions from without begin to embarrass him, and the net of circumstance to entangle him, the fatal secret struggles with still greater violence to burst forth. It must be confessed, it will be confessed; there is no refuge from confession but suicide, and suicide is confession.

Gentlemen, your whole concern in this case should be to do your duty, and let consequences take care of themselves. You will receive the law from the court. Your verdict, it is true, may endanger the prisoner's life, but then it is to save other lives. If the prisoner's guilt has been shown and proved beyond all reasonable doubt, you will convict him. If such reasonable doubt of guilt still remains, you will acquit him. You are the judges of the whole case. You owe a duty to the public as well as to the prisoner at the bar. You cannot presume to be wiser than the law. Your duty is a plain, straightforward one. Doubtless we would all judge him in mercy. Toward him as an individual the law inculcates no hostility; but toward him, if proven to be a murderer, the law, and the oaths you have taken, and public justice, demand that you do your duty.

With consciences satisfied with the discharge of duty, no consequences can harm you. There is no evil that we cannot either face or fly from but the consciousness of duty disregarded. A sense of duty pursues us ever. It is omnipresent like the Deity. If we take to ourselves the wings of the morning and dwell in the uttermost parts of the sea, duty performed, or duty violated, is still with us, for our happiness or our misery. If we say the darkness shall cover us, in the darkness as in the light our obligations are yet with us. We cannot escape their power nor fly from their presence. They are with us in this life, will be with us at its close; and in that scene of inconceivable solemnity, which lies yet farther onward, we shall still find ourselves surrounded by the consciousness of duty, to pain us wherever it has been violated, and to console us so far as God may have given us grace to perform it.

THE GREAT CHARTER.

U. M. ROSE.

Extract from a paper on " The Rise of Constitutional Law," read before the Pennsylvania State Bar Association, June 25, 1901.

No one can sum up the debt that we owe to the Magna Charta, the one great product of the Middle Ages. We look back with feelings of aversion and pity to that dark and troubled period; to its insane crusades, to its fanatical intolerance, to its pedantic and barren literature, to its scholastic disputes, to its cruelty, rapine, and bloodshed. But the genius that presides over human destiny never sleeps; and it was precisely in that most sterile and unpromising age that the groundwork was laid for all that is valuable in modern civilization. As an unborn forest sleeps unconsciously in an acorn cup, all the creations and all the potentialities of that civilization lay enfolded in the guaranty of personal liberty and of the supremacy of the law that was secured at Runnymede. The various bills and petitions of right, and the Habeas Corpus Act, while they have given new sanctions to liberty, are but echoes of the Great Charter; and our Declaration of Independence is but the Magna Charta writ large, and expanded to meet the wants of a new generation of freemen, fighting the battle of life beneath other skies.

"Worth all the classics!" Yes, the classics that have survived and the classics that have perished. Dear as might be to us the lost books of Livy, whose pictured page is torn just where its highest interest begins, or even some song of Homer, which, now lost in space, shall charm the ear and bewitch the human heart no more, we could not exchange for them a single word of those uncouth but grand old sentences, which, having taken the wings of the morning, have incorporated themselves with almost every system of laws in Christendom, and which still ring out in our American constitutions with a sound like that of the trampling of armed men, marching confidently up to battle; words which for ages have stayed the hand of tyranny, and which have extended their protection over the infant sleeping in its cradle, over the lonely, the desolate, the sorrowful, and the oppressed. Uttered by unwilling lips, and believed by the wretch from whom it was extorted that it had scarcely an hour to live, the Magna Charta marks an epoch in the annals of mankind. It began a revolution that has never gone backward for a single moment; and was the precursor of that civilization the dawn of which our eyes have looked upon with joy and pride, and whose full meridian splendor can be foreseen by God alone.

TRAINING FOR THE LEGAL PROFESSION.

EDWARD J. PHELPS.

Extract from an address to the graduating class of the Boston University School of Law, June 3, 1879.

The success of the lawyer in the long run, and the best run, and the only run that is worth regarding, is exactly commensurate with his absolute, unflexible, unqualified devotion to the truth. The world has amused itself, and I suppose will continue to amuse itself, with a good deal of cheap wit on this subject. Many people think the lawyer has nothing to do with the truth; that his business is to pervert it, to distort it, to evade it, to crown it with the thorns of all manner of technicalities, and to crucify it between two thieves. Well, that is very amusing, doubtless; but it is a serious mistake. For your success, I repeat, will be in proportion to the extent to which you become, not only the students, but the champions, the advocates, the living examples, in all respects and particulars, of *the truth.*

Another great requisite of the lawyer is that rare quality that may be called intellectual honesty. It is a mental and not a moral quality. Of course, it is one which involves high moral integrity. But those who are honest in intentions and purposes, merely, may fall far short of it. By "intellectual honesty" I mean the faculty of seeing things just as they are, — unmoved by prejudice, or passion, or excitement, or clamor, — seeing them, and reaching conclusions in regard to them, in a straightforward and direct way. That is the leading characteristic of every great lawyer or great judge that has ever lived, and the want of it is the reason the world has seen so many good lawyers and good judges and so few great ones. It is the rarest of qualities in its perfection, and the first to be recognized by mankind when it exists. Perhaps the most illustrious example there has ever been, among many illustrious examples of that quality, was Chief Justice Marshall — that magistrate of all magistrates — whose splendid judgments have entered, not only into the jurisprudence, but into the history and literature of our country. When the construction of the American Constitution was a thing of doubt; when the Constitution itself — its success, its practicability — was questioned; when men's minds were wrought up to the highest

pitch of political and personal excitement, those great judgments of Marshall and his compeers ended all dispute. No
man went away cursing the court and resolved to renew the
quarrel. The defeated side went away admitting that they
had been mistaken. That illustrates the idea that I advanced just now: that this quality, when it exists in a high
degree, is universally recognized by mankind and commands
immediate confidence.

Finally, no lawyer can attain the highest rank in his profession unless he is an effective speaker. Ideas, if they are
to be expressed, and enforced, and maintained, require the
means of expression. Advocacy, in its lawyer-like sense,
in the sense that courts of justice and competent lawyers
appreciate, means the power of clear and lucid statement,
cogent, effective, effectual reasoning, pertinent illustration,
felicitous presentation. What it does not mean, but
what a great many people seem to think it does mean, is
the everlasting *talk* of the men who have nothing to say.
Certainly, the first requisite of the successful speaker is
to have something to say. Until a man is furnished with
ideas, there is no precedent justifying the opening of his
mouth. If there is any nuisance more insufferable than all
other insufferable nuisances, it is that advocate — the terror
of unhappy courts of justice — who is popularly said to
have the "gift of gab," that is, the faculty of talking when
he has nothing to say. It is a faculty which, unlike the
quality of unstrained mercy, *curses* "him that gives as well
as him that receives." Still, it remains true, after all has
been said, that the advocate who is going to be heard "when
anvils ring and hammers beat," who is to be the champion
of a great cause on a great occasion, must be furnished with

something besides legal knowledge. He wants language. Language is to the speaker what color is to the painter — the vehicle. He wants the capacity of reasoning, of stating, of illustrating, of carrying the minds of his hearers with him. Now, that power may come by nature to some men, as Judge Dogberry thought reading and writing did; but I never met such an instance. When you find a man possessing that gift, a man who is always going to be attended to when he speaks, and who is likely to be successful, on the right side at least, when he addresses an intelligent tribunal, you will find that he has somewhere and somehow filled and stored his mind with the culture of fine letters and literature. Reason, logic, and learning hew the way, but advocacy illuminates. It is a calcium light that points the way that reason hews out through the rocks, so that the wayfaring man may see it.

GETTYSBURG ADDRESS.

ABRAHAM LINCOLN.

Delivered upon the occasion of the dedication of Gettysburg Cemetery.

Fourscore and seven years ago our fathers brought forth upon this continent a new nation, conceived in liberty and dedicated to the proposition that all men are created equal. Now we are engaged in a great civil war, testing whether that nation — or any nation so conceived and so dedicated — can long endure.

We are met on a great battle-field of that war. We are met to dedicate a portion of it as the final resting-place of those who have given their lives that that nation might live.

It is altogether fitting and proper that we should do this. But in a larger sense we cannot dedicate, we cannot consecrate, we cannot hallow, this ground. The brave men, living and dead, who struggled here, have consecrated it far above our power to add or to detract. The world will very little note, nor long remember, what we say here; but it can never forget what they did here.

It is for us, the living, rather, to be dedicated here, to the unfinished work that they have thus far so nobly carried on. It is rather for us to be here dedicated to the great task remaining before us; that from these honored dead we take increased devotion to that cause for which they here gave the last full measure of devotion; that we here highly resolve that these dead shall not have died in vain; that the nation shall, under God, have a new birth of freedom, and that government of the people, by the people, for the people, shall not perish from the earth.

ABRAHAM LINCOLN.

HENRY WATTERSON.

Extract from his oration on Lincoln, first delivered at the Auditorium, Chicago, February 12, 1895.

From Cæsar to Bismarck and Gladstone the world has had its statesmen and its soldiers — men who rose to eminence step by step, through a series of geometric progression, as it were, each advancement following in regular order one after the other, the whole obedient to well-established and well-understood laws of cause and effect. They were not what we call "men of destiny." They were "men of the time." They were men whose careers had a beginning, a middle, and an end, rounding off lives with histories, full, it may be, of interesting and exciting event, but comprehensive and comprehensible,— simple, clear, complete.

The inspired ones are fewer. Whence their emanation, where and how they got their power, by what rule they lived, moved, and had their being, we know not. There is no explication to their lives. They rose from shadow, and they went in mist. We see them, feel them, but we know them not. They came, God's word upon their lips; they did their office, God's mantle about them; and they vanished, God's holy light between the world and them, leaving behind a memory, half mortal and half myth. From first to last they were the creations of some special Providence, baffling the wit of man to fathom, defeating the machinations of the world, the flesh, and the devil, until their work was done, then passing from the scene as mysteriously as they had come upon it.

Tried by this standard, where shall we find an example so impressive as Abraham Lincoln, whose career might be chanted by a Greek chorus as at once the prelude and the epilogue of the most imperial theme of modern times?

Born as lowly as the Son of God, in a hovel; reared in penury, squalor, with no gleam of light or fair surrounding; without graces, actual or acquired; without name or fame or official training; it was reserved for this strange being, late in life, to be snatched from obscurity, raised to supreme command at a supreme moment, and intrusted with the destiny of a nation.

The great leaders of his party, the most experienced and accomplished public men of the day, were made to stand aside; were sent to the rear, whilst this fantastic figure was led by unseen hands to the front and given the reins of power. It is immaterial whether we were for him or against him,—wholly immaterial. That, during four years, carrying with them such a weight of responsibility as the world never witnessed before, he filled the vast space allotted him in the eyes and actions of mankind, is to say that he was inspired of God, for nowhere else could he have acquired the wisdom and the virtue.

Where did Shakspeare get his genius? Where did Mozart get his music? Whose hand smote the lyre of the Scottish ploughman, and stayed the life of the German priest? God, and God alone; and as surely as these were raised up by God, inspired by God, was Abraham Lincoln; and a thousand years hence, no drama, no tragedy, no epic poem will be filled with greater wonder, or be followed by mankind with deeper feeling, than that which tells the story of his life and death.

ROBERT E. LEE.

JOHN W. DANIEL.

Extract from an oration delivered at the unveiling of the recumbent figure of General Lee, at Washington and Lee University, Lexington, Virginia, June 28, 1883.

In personal appearance General Lee was a man whom once to see was ever to remember. His figure was tall, erect, well proportioned, lithe, and graceful. A fine head, with broad, uplifted brows, and features boldly yet delicately chiselled, bore the aspect of one born to command.

His whole countenance bespoke alike a powerful mind and an indomitable will, yet beamed with charity, benevolence, and gentleness. In his manners quiet reserve, unaffected courtesy, and native dignity made manifest the character of one who can only be described by the name of gentleman.

Mounted in the field and at the head of his troops, a glimpse of Lee was an inspiration. His figure was as distinctive as that of Napoleon. The black slouch hat, the cavalry boots, the dark cape, the plain gray coat without an ornament but the three stars on the collar, the calm, victorious face, the splendid, manly figure on the gray war-horse, — he looked every inch the true knight — the grand, invincible champion of a great principle.

The men who wrested victory from his little band stood wonder-stricken and abashed when they saw how few were those who dared oppose them, and generous admiration burst into spontaneous tribute to the splendid leader who bore defeat with the quiet resignation of a hero. The men who fought under him never revered or loved him more than on the day he sheathed his sword. Had he but said the word, they would have died for honor. It was because he said the word that they resolved to live for duty.

Plato congratulated himself, first, that he was born a man; second, that he had the happiness of being a Greek; and third, that he was a contemporary of Sophocles. And in this audience to-day, and here and there the wide world over, is many an one who wore the gray, who rejoices that he was born a man to do a man's part for his suffering country; that he had the glory of being a Confederate; and who feels a justly proud and glowing consciousness in his bosom when he says unto himself, "I was a follower of

Robert E. Lee. I was a soldier in the army of Northern Virginia."

As president of Washington and Lee University, General Lee exhibited qualities not less worthy and heroic than those displayed on the broad and open theatre of conflict when the eyes of nations watched his every action. In the quiet walks of academic life, far removed from "war or battle's sound," came into view the towering grandeur, the massive splendor, and the loving kindness of his character. There he revealed in manifold gracious hospitalities, tender charities, and patient, worthy counsels, how deep and pure and inexhaustible were the fountains of his virtues. And loving hearts delight to recall, as loving lips will ever delight to tell, the thousand little things he did which sent forth lines of light to irradiate the gloom of the conquered land and to lift up the hopes and cheer the works of his people.

Come we then to-day in loyal love to sanctify our memories, to purify our hopes, to make strong all good intent by communion with the spirit of him who, being dead, yet speaketh. Let us crown his tomb with the oak, the emblem of his strength, and with the laurel, the emblem of his glory. And as we seem to gaze once more on him we loved and hailed as Chief, the tranquil face is clothed with heaven's light, and the mute lips seem eloquent with the message that in life he spoke, "There is a true glory and a true honor; the glory of duty done, the honor of the integrity of principle."

STONEWALL JACKSON.

MOSES D. HOGE.

The day after the first battle of Manassas, and before the history of that victory had reached Lexington in authentic form, a crowd had gathered around the post-office, awaiting with intensest interest the opening of the mail. In its distribution the first letter was handed to the Rev. Dr. White. Recognizing at a glance the well-known super-scription, the doctor exclaimed to those around him, "Now we shall know all the facts."

The letter was from General Jackson; but instead of a war bulletin, it was a simple note, inclosing a check for a colored Sunday-school, with an apology for his delay in not sending it before. Not a word about the conflict which had electrified a nation! Not an allusion to the splendid part he had taken in it; not a reference to himself, beyond the fact that it had been to him a fatiguing day's service! And yet that was the day ever memorable in his history, when he received the name of "Stonewall" Jackson.

When his brigade of twenty-six hundred men had for hours withstood the iron tempest which broke upon it; when the Confederate right had been overwhelmed in the rush of resistless numbers, General Bee rode up to Jackson, and, with despairing bitterness, exclaimed, "General, they are beating us back!" "Then," said Jackson, calm and curt, "we will give them the bayonet." Bee seemed to catch the inspiration of his determined will; and galloping back to the broken fragments of his overtaxed command, exclaimed, "There is Jackson, standing like a stone wall.

Rally behind him, Virginians!" From that time Jackson's was known as the Stonewall Brigade — a name henceforth immortal, for the christening was baptized in the blood of its author; and that wall of brave hearts was, on every battle-field, a steadfast bulwark of their country.

In the state where all that is mortal of this great hero sleeps, there is a natural bridge of rock, whose massive arch, fashioned in grandeur by the hand of God, springs lightly toward the sky, spanning a chasm into whose awful depths the beholder looks down bewildered and awe-struck. But its grandeur is not diminished because tender vines clamber over its gigantic piers and sweet-scented flowers nestle in its crevices. Nor is the granite strength of Jackson's character weakened because in every throb of his heart there was a pulsation ineffably and exquisitely tender. The hum of bees, the fragrance of clover fields, the tender streaks of dawn, the dewy brightness of early spring, the mellow glories of matured autumn, all by turns charmed and tranquillized him. The eye that flashed amid the smoke of battle grew soft in contemplating the beauty of a flower. The ear that thrilled with the thunder of the cannonade drank in with innocent delight the song of birds and the prattle of children's voices. The voice whose sharp and ringing tones had so often uttered the command, " Give them the bayonet," called even from foreign tongues terms of endearment for those he loved; and the man who filled two hemispheres with his fame was never so happy as when he was telling the colored children of his Sabbath-school the story of the Cross.

Standing before this statue, as in the living presence of the man it represents; cordially indorsing, as we do, the principles of the political school in which he was trained, and in defence of which he died, and unable yet to think of our dead Confederacy without memories unutterably tender, I speak not for myself, but for the South, when I say it is our interest, our duty, and determination to maintain the Union, and to make every possible contribution to its prosperity and glory, if all the states which compose it will unite in making it such a Union as our fathers framed, and enthroning above it the Constitution in its old supremacy. If ever these states are welded together in one great, fraternal, and enduring Union, with one heart pulsating through the entire frame, as the tides throb through the bosom of the sea, it will be when they all stand on the same level, with such a jealous regard for one another's rights, that when the interests or honor of one are assailed, all the rest, feeling the wound, will kindle with just resentment at the outrage. But if that cannot be, then I trust the day will never dawn when the Southern people will add degradation to defeat, and hypocrisy to subjugation, by professing a love for the Union which denies to one of their states a single right accorded to Massachusetts or New York. To such a Union we will never be heartily loyal while that bronze hand grasps the sword, while yonder river chants the requiem of the sixteen thousand Confederate dead who sleep on the hills of Hollywood.

THE SOLDIER'S LAST SALUTE.

HORACE PORTER.

On the morning of Decoration Day, 1885, the Grand Army of the Republic, the veterans in the vicinity of New York

City who had served under General Grant, rose earlier than was their wont, spent more time than usual in unfurling their old battle-flags, and in burnishing the medals of honor which decorated their breasts; for they had resolved on that day to march by the house of their dying commander, and give him one last marching salute.

Outside that house the street was filled with marching men and martial music. Inside that house the old chief lay on a bed of anguish, the pallor of death already beginning to overspread his illustrious features. The hand which had seized the surrendered swords of countless thousands was scarcely able to return the pressure of a friendly grasp; the voice which had cheered on to triumphant victory the legions of American manhood was no longer able to call for the cooling draught which slaked the thirst of a fevered tongue. And prostrate upon that bed of suffering lay the form which in the new world had ridden at the head of conquering columns; in the old world had marched through the palaces of crowned heads with the descendants of a line of kings rising and standing uncovered in his presence.

His ear caught the sound of the movement of marching men. The bands were playing the grand strains which had mingled with the echo of his guns at Vicksburg, playing the same quicksteps to which his men had sped in hot haste in pursuit of Lee through Virginia; and then came the steady, measured, swinging step of war-trained men, which seemed to shake the earth. He understood it all then. It was the tread of his old veterans. He seized his crutch and dragged himself painfully and slowly to the window. As he saw those old battle-flags dipping to him in salute, he once more drew himself into the position of a soldier; and as he gazed upon those banners, bullet-ridden and battle-stained, many of them but a remnant of their former selves, there kindled in his eyes the flames which had lighted them at Chattanooga, in the Wilderness, amidst the glories of Appomattox; and as those veterans bared their heads to that May morning's breeze, and looked for the last time with upturned eyes on their old chief, cheeks which had been bronzed by southern suns and begrimed with powder were now bathed in tears of manly grief. And then they saw the rising hand which had so often pointed out to them the path of victory. He raised it slowly and feebly to his head in acknowledgment of their salutations. The last of the column passed. The hand fell heavily by his side. It was the soldier's last salute.

THE DEATH OF GARFIELD.

JAMES G. BLAINE.

Extract from a speech delivered in Congress, February 26, 1882.

On the morning of Saturday, July 2, 1881, President Garfield was a contented and happy man — not in an ordinary degree, but joyfully, almost boyishly happy. And surely, if happiness can ever come from the honors or triumphs of this world, on that quiet July morning Garfield may well have been a happy man. No foreboding of evil haunted him; no premonition of danger clouded his sky. One moment he stood erect, strong, confident in the years stretching peacefully out before him; the next he lay wounded, bleeding, helpless, doomed to weary weeks of torture, to silence, and the grave.

Great in life, he was surpassingly great in death. For no cause, in the very frenzy of wantonness and wickedness, by the red hand of murder, he was thrust from the full tide of this world's interests, from its hopes, its aspirations, its victories, into the visible presence of death — and he did not quail. Not alone for the one short moment in which, stunned and dazed, he could give up life, hardly aware of its relinquishment, but through days of deadly languor, through weeks of agony that was not less agony because silently borne, with clear sight and calm courage, he looked into his open grave.

As the end drew near, his early craving for the sea returned. The stately mansion of power had become to him the wearisome hospital of pain, and he begged to be taken from its prison walls, from its oppressive, stifling air, from its homelessness and its hopelessness. Gently, silently, the love of a great people bore the pale sufferer to the longed-for healing of the sea, to live or to die, as God should will, within sight of its heaving billows, within sound of its manifold voices. With wan, fevered face tenderly lifted to the cooling breeze, he looked out wistfully upon the ocean's changing wonders: on its far sails, whitening in the morning light; on its restless waves, rolling shoreward to break and die beneath the noonday sun; on the red clouds of evening, arching low to the horizon; on the serene and shining pathway of the stars.

Let us think that his dying eyes read a mystic meaning which only the rapt and parting soul may know. Let us believe that in the silence of the receding world he heard the great waves breaking on a farther shore, and felt already upon his wasted brow the breath of the eternal morning.

WILLIAM McKINLEY.

JOHN HAY.

Extract from a eulogy delivered at the official exercises commemorative of President McKinley.

For the third time the Congress of the United States are assembled to commemorate the life and death of a President slain by the hand of an assassin. The attention of the future historian will be attracted to the features which reappear with startling sameness in all three of these awful crimes: the uselessness, the utter lack of consequence of the act; the obscurity, the insignificance of the criminal; the blamelessness — so far as in our sphere of existence the best of men may be held blameless — of the victim. Not one of our murdered presidents had an enemy in the world; they were all of such preëminent purity of life that no pretext could be given for the attack of passional crime; they were all men of democratic instincts who could never have offended the most jealous advocates of equality; they were of kindly and generous nature, to whom wrong or injustice was impossible; of moderate fortune, whose slender means nobody could envy. They were men of austere virtue, of tender heart, of eminent abilities, which they had devoted with single minds to the good of the Republic. If ever men walked before God and man without blame, it was these three rulers of our people. The only temptation to attack their lives offered was their gentle radiance — to eyes hating the light, that was offence enough.

In a mood of high hope, of generous expectation, President McKinley went to Buffalo, and there, on the threshold of eternity, he delivered that memorable speech, worthy for its loftiness of tone, its blameless morality, its breadth of view, to be regarded as his testament to the nation. Through all his pride of country and his joy of its success runs the note of solemn warning, as in Kipling's noble hymn, "Lest we forget." Nothing I might say could give such a picture of the President's mind and character. His years of apprenticeship had been served. He stood that day past master of the art of statesmanship. He had nothing more to ask of the people. He owed them nothing but truth and faithful service. His mind and heart were purged of the temptations which beset all men engaged in the struggle to survive. In view of the revelation of his nature vouchsafed to us that day, and the fate which impended over him, we can only say in deep affection and solemn awe, "Blessed are the pure in heart, for they shall see God." Even for that vision he was not unworthy.

He had not long to wait. The next day sped the bolt of doom, and for a week after — in an agony of dread broken by illusive glimpses of hope that our prayers might be answered — the nation waited for the end. Nothing in the glorious life that we saw gradually waning was more admirable and exemplary than its close. The gentle humanity of his words when he saw his assailant in danger of summary vengeance, "Don't let them hurt him"; his chivalrous care that the news should be broken gently to his wife; the fine courtesy with which he apologized for the damage which his death would bring to the great exhibition; and the heroic resignation of his final words, "It is God's way; His will, not ours, be done," were all the instinctive expressions of a nature so lofty and so pure that pride in its nobility at once softened and enhanced the nation's sense of loss.

The obvious elements which enter into the fame of a public man are few and by no means recondite. The man who fills a great station in a period of change, who leads his country successfully through a time of crisis; who, by his power of persuading and controlling others, has been able to command the best thought of his age, so as to leave his country in a moral or material condition in advance of where he found it — such a man's position in history is secure. If, in addition to this, his written or spoken words possess the subtle quality which carry them far and lodge them in men's hearts; and, more than all, if his utterances and actions, while informed with a lofty morality, are yet tinged with the glow of human sympathy, the fame of such a man will shine like a beacon through the mists of ages — an object of reverence, of imitation, and of love.

It should be to us an occasion of solemn pride that in the three great crises of our history such a man was not denied us. The moral value to a nation of a renown such as Washington's and Lincoln's and McKinley's is beyond all computation. No loftier ideal can be held up to the emulation of ingenuous youth. With such examples we cannot be wholly ignoble. Grateful as we may be for what they did, let us be still more grateful for what they were. While our daily being, our public policies, still feel the influence of their work, let us pray that in our spirits their lives may be voluble, calling us upward and onward.

There is not one of us but feels prouder of his native land because the august figure of Washington presided over its beginnings; no one but vows it a tenderer love because

Lincoln poured out his blood for it; no one but must feel his devotion for his country renewed and kindled when he remembers how McKinley loved, revered, and served it, showed in his life how a citizen should live, and in his last hour taught us how a gentleman could die.

THE NEW SOUTH.

HENRY W. GRADY.

Extract from the speech that first brought him national fame as an orator. Delivered at a dinner of the New England Society, New York City, December 26, 1886.

" There was a South of slavery and secession — that South is dead. There is a South of union and freedom — that South, thank God, is living, breathing, growing every hour." - These words, delivered from the immortal lips of Benjamin H. Hill, at Tammany Hall, in 1866, true then, and truer now, I shall make my text to-night.

Dr. Talmage has drawn for you, with a master hand, the picture of your returning armies. He has told you how, in the pomp and circumstance of war, they came back to you, marching with proud and victorious tread, reading their glory in a nation's eyes! Will you bear with me while I tell you of another army that sought its home at the close of the late war? An army that marched home in defeat and not in victory — in pathos and not in splendor, but in glory that equalled yours, and to hearts as loving as ever welcomed heroes home. Let me picture to you the footsore Confederate soldier, as, buttoning up in his faded gray jacket the parole which was to bear testimony to his children

of his fidelity and faith, he turned his face southward from
Appomattox in April, 1865! Think of him as ragged, half-
starved, heavy-hearted, enfeebled by want and wounds;
having fought to exhaustion, he surrenders his gun, wrings
the hand of his comrade in silence, and, lifting his tear-
stained and pallid face for the last time to the graves that
dot the old Virginia hills, pulls his gray cap over his brow,
and begins the slow and painful journey. What does he
find? — let me ask you who went to your homes eager to
find, in the welcome you had justly earned, full payment for
four years' sacrifice — what does he find when, having followed the battle-stained cross against overwhelming odds,
dreading death not half so much as surrender, he reaches
the home he left so prosperous and beautiful? He finds his
house in ruins, his farm devastated, his slaves free, his stock
killed, his barn empty, his trade destroyed, his money worthless; his social system, feudal in its magnificence, swept
away; his people without law or legal status; his comrades
slain, and the burdens of others heavy on his shoulders.
Crushed by defeat, his very traditions gone; without money,
credit, employment, material training; and besides all this,
confronted with the gravest problem that ever met human
intelligence — the establishing of a status for the vast body
of his liberated slaves.

What does he do — this hero in gray with a heart of gold?
Does he sit down in sullenness and despair? Not for a
day. Surely God, who had stripped him of his prosperity,
inspired him in his adversity. As ruin was never before so
overwhelming, never was restoration swifter. The soldier
stepped from the trenches into the furrow; horses that had
charged Federal guns marched before the plough; and fields

that ran red with human blood in April were green with harvest in June.

But what is the sum of our work ? We have found that in the general summary the free negro counts for more than he did as a slave. We have planted the schoolhouse on the hilltop and made it free to white and black. We have sowed towns and cities in the place of theories and put business above politics.

The new South is enamoured of her new work. Her soul is stirred with the breath of a new life. The light of a grander day is falling fair on her face. She is thrilling with the consciousness of a growing power and prosperity. As she stands upright, full statured, and equal among the people of the earth, breathing the keen air and looking out upon the expanding horizon, she understands that her emancipation came because, in the inscrutable wisdom of God, her honest purpose was crossed and her brave armies beaten.

This is said in no spirit of time-serving or apology. The South has nothing for which to apologize. The South has nothing to take back. In my native town of Athens is a monument that crowns its central hills — a plain white shaft. Deep cut into its shining side is a name dear to me above the names of men, that of a brave and simple man who died in a brave and simple faith. Not for all the glories of New England — from Plymouth Rock all the way — would I exchange the heritage he left me in his soldier's death. To the feet of that shaft I shall send my children's children to reverence him who ennobled their name with his heroic blood. But, speaking from the shadow of that memory, which I honor as I do nothing else on earth, I say that the cause in which he suffered and for which he gave his life was adjudged by higher and fuller wisdom than his or mine, and I am glad that the omniscient God held the balance of battle in his almighty hand, and that human slavery was swept forever from American soil — the American Union saved from the wreck of the war.

This message comes to you from hallowed ground, — doubly hallowed by the fallen heroes who wore the gray and by those who wore the blue. Now what answer has New England to this message? Will she permit the prejudice of war to remain in the hearts of the conquerors when it has died in the hearts of the conquered? Will she transmit this prejudice to the next generation, that in their hearts, which never felt the generous ardor of conflict, it may perpetuate itself? Will she make the last words of your great chieftain — "Let us have peace" — a delusion or an inspiration? Will she withhold, save in strained courtesy, the hand which, straight from his soldier's heart, Grant offered to Lee at Appomattox? If she does, the South, never abject in asking for comradeship, must accept with dignity its refusal; but if she does not — if she accepts with frankness and sincerity this message of good-will and friendship, then will the prophecy of Webster, delivered in this very Society forty years ago, amid tremendous applause, be verified in its fullest and final sense, when he said, "Standing hand to hand and clasping hands, we should remain united as we have for sixty years, citizens of the same country, members of the same government, united all, united now, and united forever."

THE MINUTE MAN OF THE REVOLUTION.

GEORGE WILLIAM CURTIS.

Extract from an oration delivered at the centennial celebration of Concord Fight, Concord, Massachusetts, April 10, 1876. "Orations and Addresses," copyright, 1894, by Harper and Brothers.

The Minute Man of the Revolution! And who was he? He was the old, the middle-aged, and the young. He was the husband and the father, who left his plough in the furrow and his hammer on the bench, and marched to die or be free. He was the son and lover, the plain, shy youth of the singing school and the village choir, whose heart beat to arms for his country, and who felt, though he could not say with the old English cavalier: —

> "I could not love thee, dear, so much,
>   Loved I not honor more."

He was the man who was willing to pour out his life's blood for a principle. Intrenched in his own honesty, the king's gold could not buy him; enthroned in the love of his fellow-citizens, the king's writ could not take him; and when, on the morning of Lexington, the king's troops marched to seize him, his sublime faith saw, beyond the clouds of the moment, the rising sun of the America we behold, and, careless of himself, mindful only of his country, he exultingly exclaimed, "Oh, what a glorious morning!" And then amid the flashing hills, the ringing woods, the flaming roads, he smote with terror the haughty British column, and sent it shrinking, bleeding, wavering, and reeling through the streets of the village, panic-stricken and broken.

atefully recall to-day; him we commit in his
h to the reverence of our children. And here
eful fields, — here in the heart of Middlesex
County, of Lexington and Concord and Bunker Hill, stand
fast, Son of Liberty, as the minute-men stood at the old
North Bridge. But should we or our descendants, false to
justice or humanity, betray in any way their cause, spring
into life as a hundred years ago, take one more step, descend, and lead us, as God led you in saving America, to
save the hopes of man.

No hostile fleet for many a year has vexed the waters of
our coast; nor is any army but our own ever likely to tread
our soil. Not such are our enemies to-day. They do not
come, proudly stepping to the drum beat, their bayonets
flashing in the morning sun. But wherever party spirit
shall strain the ancient guarantees of freedom; or bigotry
and ignorance shall lay their fatal hands on education; or
the arrogance of caste shall strike at equal rights; or corruption shall poison the very springs of national life, —
there, Minute Man of Liberty, are your Lexington Green
and Concord Bridge. And as you love your country and
your kind, and would have your children rise up and call
you blessed, spare not the enemy. Over the hills, out of the
earth, down from the clouds, pour in resistless might. Fire
from every rock and tree, from door and window, from
hearthstone and chamber. Hang upon his flank from morn
to sunset, and so, through a land blazing with indignation,
hurl the hordes of ignorance and corruption and injustice
back — back in utter defeat and ruin.

HAPPINESS AND LIBERTY.

ROBERT G. INGERSOLL.

It is not necessary to be rich in order to be happy. The laugh of a child will brighten the gloom of the darkest day. Strike with the hand of fire, O weird musician, upon the harpstring with Apollo's golden hair. Fill the vast cathedral aisles with symphonies sweet and dim. Blow, bugles, blow until your silvery notes do touch and kiss the moonlit waves and charm the lovers wandering 'neath the vine-clad hills; but know that your sweetest strains are but discords all compared with childhood's happy laugh. Oh, rippling river of laughter, thou art the blessed boundary line between man and beast, and each wayward wave of thine doth catch and drown some fitful fiend of care!

Do not tell me you have got to be rich. We have a false standard of these things in the United States. We think that a man must be great, that he must be famous, that he must be wealthy. That is all a mistake. It is not necessary to be rich, to be great, to be famous, to be powerful, in order to be happy. The happy man is the free man. Happiness is the legal tender of the soul. Joy is wealth. Liberty is joy.

A little while ago I stood by the grave of the old Napoleon—a magnificent tomb of gilt and gold, fit almost for a dead deity—and gazed upon the sarcophagus of black Egyptian marble, where rest at last the ashes of that restless man. I leaned over the balustrade and thought about the career of the greatest soldier of the modern world.

I saw him walking upon the banks of the Seine, contemplating suicide. I saw him at Toulon — I saw him putting down the mob in the streets of Paris — I saw him at the head of the army of Italy — I saw him crossing the bridge of Lodi with the tricolor in his hand — I saw him in Egypt in the shadow of the pyramids — I saw him conquer the Alps and mingle the eagles of France with the eagles of the crags. I saw him at Marengo — at Ulm and Auster-litz. I saw him in Russia, where the infantry of the snow and the cavalry of the wild blast scattered his legions like winter's withered leaves. I saw him at Leipsic in defeat and disaster — driven by a million bayonets back upon Paris — clutched like a wild beast — banished to Elba. I saw him escape and retake an empire by the force of his genius. I saw him upon the frightful field of Waterloo, where Chance and Fate combined to wreck the fortunes of their former king. And I saw him at St. Helena, with his hands crossed behind him, gazing out upon the sad and solemn sea.

I thought of all the orphans and widows he had made — of the tears that had been shed for his glory, and of the only woman who ever loved him, pushed from his heart by the ruthless hand of ambition. And I said I would rather have been a French peasant and worn wooden shoes; I would rather have lived in a hut with the vines growing over the door and the grapes growing purple in the kisses of the autumn sun, with my loving wife knitting by my side as the day died out the sky; yes, I would rather have been that man and gone down to the tongueless silence of the dream-less dust, than to have been that imperial impersonation of force and murder known as Napoleon the Great.

No, it is not necessary to be great to be happy. It is not necessary to be rich to be generous. It is not necessary to be powerful to be just. When the world is free, this question will be settled. A new creed will be written. In that creed there will be but one word, "Liberty." O Liberty, float not forever in the far horizon, remain not forever in the dream of the enthusiast, dwell not forever in the song of the poet, but come and make thy home among the children of men. I know not what thoughts, what discoveries, what inventions may leap from the brain of man; I know not what garments of glory may be woven by the years to come; I cannot dream of the victories to be won upon the field of thought. But I do know that coming from the infinite sea of the future there shall never touch this bank and shoal of time, a richer gift, a rarer blessing, than Liberty.

REVOLUTIONS.

WENDELL PHILLIPS.

An extract from his lecture on "Public Opinion."

Whenever you meet a dozen earnest men pledged to a new idea, you meet the beginning of a new revolution. Revolutions are not made; they come. A revolution is as natural a growth as an oak. It comes out of the past; its foundations are laid far back. The child feels; he grows into a man, and thinks; another, perhaps, speaks; and the world acts out the thought. And this is the history of modern society. Men undervalue great reform movements because they imagine you can always put your finger on some illustrious moment in history and say, "Here commenced the great change which has come over the nation." Not so. The beginning of a great change is like the rising of the Mississippi. You must stoop and gather away the pebbles to find it. But soon it swells broader and broader; bears on its bosom the navies of a mighty republic; forms the gulf and divides a continent.

There is a story of Napoleon which illustrates my meaning. We are apt to trace the control of France to some noted victory; to the time when he encamped in the Tuileries, or when he dissolved the assembly by the stamp of his foot. He reigned in fact when his hand first felt the helm of the vessel of state, and that was far back of the time when he had conquered Italy, or his name had been echoed over two continents. It was on the day five hundred irresolute men were met in the assembly which called itself, and pretended to be, the government of France. They heard that the mob of Paris were coming next morning, thirty thousand strong, to turn them, as was usual in those days, out of doors. And where did this seemingly great power go for its support and refuge? They sent Tallien to seek out a boy lieutenant — the shadow of an officer — so thin and pallid that when he was placed on the stand before them, the president of the assembly, fearful, if the fate of France rested on the shrunken form, the ashen cheek, before him, that all hope was gone, asked, "Young man, can you protect the assembly?" The stern lip of the Corsican boy parted only to say, "I always do what I undertake."

Then and there Napoleon ascended his throne; and the next day from the steps of the St. Roche thundered forth the cannon which taught the mob of Paris, for the first time, that it had a master. That was the commencement of the empire.

THE NEW SOUTH AND THE RACE PROBLEM.

HENRY W. GRADY.

Extract from an address before the Boston Mercantile Association,
1889.

Whatever the future may hold for the negroes, — whether they plod along in the servitude from which they have never been lifted since the Cyrenian was laid hold upon by the Roman soldiers and made to bear the cross of the fainting Christ — whether they find homes again in Africa, and thus hasten the prophecy of the Psalmist who said, " And suddenly Ethiopia shall hold out her hands unto God" — whether, forever dislocated and separate, they remain a weak people beset by a stronger — or whether in this miraculous Republic they break through the caste of twenty centuries and, belying universal history, reach the full stature of citizenship and in peace maintain it, — we shall give them uttermost justice and abiding friendship.

And whatever we may do, into whatever seeming estrangement we may be driven, nothing shall disturb the love we bear this Republic, or mitigate our consecration to its service. I stand here to profess no new loyalty. When General Lee, whose heart was the temple of our hopes and whose arm was clothed with our strength, renewed his allegiance to this government at Appomattox, he spoke from a heart too great to be false, and he spoke for every honest man from Maryland to Texas. From that day to this, Hamilcar has nowhere in the South sworn young Hannibal to hatred and revenge, but everywhere to loyalty and to love. Witness the veteran standing at the base of the Confederate

monument, above the graves of his comrades, his empty
sleeve tossing in the April wind, adjuring the young men
about him to serve as honest and loyal citizens the government against which their fathers fought.   This message,
delivered from that sacred presence, has gone home to the
hearts of my fellows.   And I declare here, if physical
courage be always equal to human aspiration, that they
would die, if need be, to restore this Republic their fathers
fought to dissolve!

Such is this question as we see it, such is the temper
in which we approach it, such the progress made.   What
do we ask of you?   First, patience; second, confidence;
third, sympathy; fourth, loyalty to the Republic—for
there is sectionalism in loyalty as in estrangement.   This
hour little needs the loyalty that is loyal to one section,
while it holds the other in enduring suspicion and estrangement.   Give us the broad and perfect loyalty that loves and
trusts Georgia alike with Massachusetts — that "knows no
South, no North, no East, no West," but endears with equal
and patriotic love every foot of our soil, every state of our
Union.

A mighty duty and a mighty inspiration impels every
one of us to lose in patriotic consecration whatever estranges,
whatever divides.   We are Americans, and we fight for
human liberty!   The uplifting force of the American idea
is under every throne on earth.   France, Brazil — these are
our victories.   To redeem the earth from kingcraft and
oppression — this is our mission!   And we shall not fail.
God has sown in our soil the seed of his millennial harvest,
and He will not apply the sickle to the ripening crop until
His full and perfect day has come.   Our history has

been a constant and expanding miracle from Plymouth Rock and Jamestown all the way — aye, even from the hour when from the voiceless and trackless ocean a new world rose to the sight of the inspired sailor.   As we approach the fourth centennial of that stupendous day, — when the old world will come to marvel and to learn, — amid our gathered pleasures let us resolve to crown the miracles of our past with the spectacle of a Republic compact, united, indissoluble in the bonds of love — serene and resplendent at the summit of human achievement and earthly glory — blazing out the path and making clear the way up which all the nations of the earth must come in God's appointed time!

ENGLAND AND THE AMERICAN COLONIES.

EDMUND BURKE.

Extract from the peroration of Burke's speech on " Conciliation with the Colonies," delivered in the House of Commons, March 22, 1775.

My hold of the colonies is in the close affection which grows from common names, from kindred blood, from similar privileges, and equal protection.   These are ties, which, though light as air, yet are as strong as links of iron. Let the colonists always keep the idea of their civil rights associated with your government, — they will cling and grapple to you, and no force under heaven will be of power to tear them from their allegiance.   But let it be once understood that your government may be one thing, and their privileges another, that these two things may exist without any mutual relation, — the cement is gone, the cohesion is loosened; and everything hastens to decay and dissolution.

As long as you have the wisdom to keep the sovereign authority of this country as the sanctuary of liberty, wherever that chosen race — the sons of England — worship freedom, they will turn their faces toward you. The more they multiply, the more friends you will have; the more ardently they love liberty, the more perfect will be their obedience. Slavery they can have anywhere; it is a weed that grows in every soil. But until you become lost to all feeling of your true interest and your natural dignity, freedom they can have from none but you. This is the commodity of price, of which you have the monopoly. This is the true Act of Navigation, which binds to you the commerce of the colonies, and, through them, secures to you the wealth of the world. It is the spirit of the English constitution, which, infused through the mighty mass, pervades, feeds, unites, invigorates, vivifies every part of the empire, even down to the minutest member.

Is it not the same virtue which does everything for us here in England? Do you imagine that it is the Land-tax Act which raises your revenue? that it is the annual vote in the Committee of Supply which gives you your army? or that it is the Mutiny Bill which inspires it with bravery and discipline? No! surely no! It is the love of the people; it is their attachment to their government, from the sense of the deep stake they have in such a glorious institution, which gives you your army and your navy, and infuses into both that liberal obedience without which your army would be a base rabble, and your navy nothing but rotten timber

A MESSAGE TO GARCIA.

ELBERT HUBBARD.

Extract from an article in the " Philistine" for March, 1899.

When war broke out between Spain and the United States, it was very necessary to communicate quickly with the leader of the Insurgents. Garcia was somewhere in the mountain fastnesses of Cuba — no one knew where. No mail or telegraph message could reach him. The President must secure his coöperation, and quickly.

What to do!

Some one said to the President, " There's a fellow by the name of Rowan will find Garcia for you if anybody can." Rowan was sent for and given a letter to be delivered to Garcia. How " the fellow by the name of Rowan" took the letter, sealed it up in an oilskin pouch, strapped it over his heart, in four days landed by night off the coast of Cuba from an open boat, disappeared into the jungle, and in three weeks came out on the other side of the island, having traversed a hostile country on foot, and delivered his letter to Garcia, are things I have no special desire now to tell in detail.

The point I wish to make is this : McKinley gave Rowan a letter to be delivered to Garcia; Rowan took the letter and did not ask, " Where is he at? " By the Eternal! there is a man whose form should be cast in deathless bronze and the statue placed in every college of the land. It is not book-learning young men need, nor instruction about this and that, but a stiffening of the vertebræ which will cause them to be loyal to a trust, to act promptly, concentrate their energies; do the thing — "Carry a message to Garcia!"

General Garcia is dead now, but there are other Garcias. No man who has endeavored to carry out an enterprise where many hands were needed, but has been well-nigh appalled at times by the imbecility of the average man — the inability or unwillingness to concentrate on a thing and do it. Slip-shod assistance, foolish inattention, dowdy indifference, and half-hearted work seem the rule; and no man succeeds, unless by hook or crook, or threat, he forces or bribes other men to assist him; or mayhap, God in His goodness performs a miracle, and sends him an angel of light for an assistant.

And this incapacity for independent action, this moral stupidity, this infirmity of the will, this unwillingness to cheerfully catch hold and lift, are the things that put pure socialism so far into the future. If men will not act for themselves, what will they do when the benefit of their effort is for all?

My heart goes out to the man who does his work when the "boss" is away, as well as when he is at home. And the man, who, when given a letter for Garcia, quietly takes the missive, without asking any idiotic questions, and with no lurking intention of chucking it into the nearest sewer, or of doing aught else but deliver it, never gets "laid off," nor has to go on a strike for higher wages. Civilization is one long anxious search for just such individuals. Anything such a man asks shall be granted; his kind is so rare that no employer can afford to let him go. He is wanted in every city, town, and village — in every office, shop, store, and factory. The world cries out for such; he is needed, and needed badly — the man who can carry a message to Garcia.

COLUMBUS.

CHAUNCEY M. DEPEW.

God always has in training some commanding genius for the control of great crises in the affairs of nations and peoples. The number of these leaders is less than the centuries, but their lives are the history of human progress. Though Cæsar, and Charlemagne, and Hildebrand, and Luther, and William the Conqueror, and Oliver Cromwell, and all the epoch-makers prepared Europe for the event, and contributed to the result, the lights which illumine our firmament to-day are Columbus the discoverer, Washington the founder, and Lincoln the saviour.

It was a happy omen of the position which woman was to hold in America that the only person who comprehended the majestic scope of his plans and the invincible quality of his genius, was the able and gracious Queen of Castile. Isabella alone of all the dignitaries of that age shares with Columbus the honors of his great achievement. She arrayed her kingdom and her private fortune behind the enthusiasm of this mystic mariner, and posterity pays homage to her wisdom and faith.

The overthrow of the Mahometan power in Spain would have been a forgotten scene in one of the innumerable acts in the grand drama of history, had not Isabella conferred immortality upon herself, her husband, and their dual crown, by her recognition of Columbus. The devout spirit of the queen and the high purpose of the explorer inspired the voyage, subdued the mutinous crew, and prevailed over the raging storms. They covered with divine radiance of religion and humanity the degrading search for gold and the horrors of its quest, which filled the first century of conquest with every form of lust and greed.

The mighty soul of the great admiral was undaunted by the ingratitude of princes and the hostility of the people, by imprisonment and neglect. He died as he was securing the means and preparing a campaign for the rescue of the Holy Sepulchre at Jerusalem from the infidel. He did not know, what time has revealed, that, while the mission of the crusades of Godfrey of Bouillon and Richard of the Lion Heart was a bloody and fruitless romance, the discovery of America was the salvation of the world. The one was the symbol, the other the spirit; the one death, the other life. The tomb of the Saviour was a narrow and empty vault, precious only for its memories of the supreme tragedy of the centuries; but the new continent was to be the home and temple of the living God.

All hail, Columbus, discoverer, dreamer, hero, and apostle! We here, of every race and country, recognize the horizon which bounded his vision and the infinite scope of his genius. The voice of gratitude and praise for all the blessings which have been showered upon mankind by adventure is limited to no language, but is uttered in every tongue. Neither marble nor brass can fitly form his statue. Continents are his monuments, and innumerable millions, past, present, and to come, who enjoy in their liberties and their happiness the fruits of his faith, will reverently guard and preserve, from century to century, his name and fame.

THE PILGRIMS.

EDWARD EVERETT.

From the dark portals of the Star Chamber and in the stern text of the Acts of Uniformity the Pilgrims received a commission more important than any that ever bore the royal seal. Their banishment to Holland was fortunate; the decline of their little company in the strange land was fortunate; the difficulties which they experienced in getting the royal consent to banish themselves to this wilderness were fortunate; all the tears and heart-breakings of that ever memorable parting at Delfshaven had the happiest influence on the rising destinies of New England. These rough touches of fortune brushed off the light, uncertain, selfish spirits; they made it a grave, solemn, self-denying expedition. They cast a broad shadow of thought and seriousness over the cause; and if this sometimes deepened into severity and bitterness, can we find no apology for such a human weakness?

Their trials of wandering and exile, of the ocean, the winter, the wilderness, and the savage foe, were the final assurance of success. They kept far away from the enterprise all patrician softness, all hereditary claims to pre-eminence. No effeminate nobility crowded into the dark and austere ranks of the Pilgrims; no Carr or Villiers desired to lead on the ill-provided band of despised Puritans; no well-endowed clergy were anxious to quit their cathedrals and set up a pompous hierarchy in the frozen wilderness; no craving governors were on the alert to be sent over to our cheerless El Dorados of ice and snow:

no; they could not say they had encouraged, patronized, or helped the Pilgrims; they could not afterwards fairly pretend to reap where they had not strown. And as our fathers reared this broad and solid fabric unaided, barely tolerated, it did not fall when the favor, which had always been withholden, was changed into wrath; when the arm, which had never supported, was raised to destroy.

Shut now the volume of history, and tell me, on any principle of human probability, what shall be the fate of this handful of adventurers. Tell me, man of military science, in how many months were they all swept off by the thirty savage tribes enumerated within the early limits of New England? Tell me, politician, how long did this shadow of a colony, on which your conventions and treaties had not smiled, languish on the distant coast? Student of history, compare for me the baffled projects, the deserted settlements, the abandoned adventures of other times, and find the parallel of this. Was it the winter's storm, beating upon the houseless heads of women and children? Was it disease? Was it the tomahawk? Was it the deep malady of a blighted hope, a ruined enterprise, and a broken heart aching in its last moments at the recollection of the loved and left beyond the sea? — Was it some or all of these united that hurried this forsaken company to their melancholy fate? And is it possible that neither of these causes, that not all combined, were able to blast this bud of hope? Is it possible that from a beginning so feeble, so frail, so worthy not so much of admiration as of pity, there has gone forth a progress so steady, a growth so wonderful. a reality so important, a promise, yet to be fulfilled, so glorious?

TRIBUTE TO LINCOLN.

EMILIO CASTELAR.

The Puritans are the patriarchs of liberty; they opened a new world on the earth; they opened a new path for the human conscience; they created a new society. Yet, when England tried to subdue them and they conquered, the Republic triumphed and slavery remained. Washington could emancipate only his own slaves. Franklin said that the Virginians could not invoke the name of God, retaining slavery. Jay said that all the prayers America sent up to heaven for the preservation of liberty while slavery continued were mere blasphemies. Mason mourned over the payment his descendants must make for this great crime of their fathers. Jefferson traced the line where the black wave of slavery should be stayed.

Nevertheless, slavery increased continually. I beg that you will pause a moment to consider the man who cleansed this terrible stain which obscured the stars of the American banner. I beg that you will pause a moment, for his immortal name has been invoked for the perpetuation of slavery. Ah! the past century has not, the century to come will not have, a figure so grand, because as evil disappears so disappears heroism also.

I have often contemplated and described his life. Born in a cabin of Kentucky, of parents who could hardly read; born a new Moses in the solitude of the desert, where are forged all great and obstinate thoughts, monotonous like the desert, and, like the desert, sublime; growing up among those primeval forests, which, with their fragrance, send a cloud of incense, and, with their murmurs, a cloud of prayers to heaven; a boatman at eight years in the impetuous current of the Ohio, and at seventeen in the vast and tranquil waters of the Mississippi; later, a woodman, with axe and arm felling the immemorial trees, to open a way to unexplored regions for his tribe of wandering workers; reading no other book than the Bible, the book of great sorrows and great hopes, dictated often by prophets to the sound of fetters they dragged through Nineveh and Babylon; a child of Nature, in a word, by one of those miracles only comprehensible among free peoples, he fought for the country, and was raised by his fellow-citizens to the Congress at Washington, and by the nation to the presidency of the Republic; and when the evil grew more virulent, when those states were dissolved, when the slaveholders uttered their war-cry and the slaves their groans of despair — the wood-cutter, the boatman, the son of the great West, the descendant of Quakers, humblest of the humble before his conscience, greatest of the great before history, ascends the Capitol, the greatest moral height of our time, and strong and serene with his conscience and his thought, — before him a veteran army, hostile Europe behind him, England favoring the South, France encouraging reaction in Mexico, in his hands the riven country, — he arms two millions of men, gathers a half million of horses, sends his artillery twelve hundred miles in a week, from the banks of the Potomac to the shores of Tennessee; fights more than six hundred battles; renews before Richmond the deeds of Alexander, of Cæsar; and, after having emancipated three million slaves, that nothing might be wanting, he dies in the very moment of victory — like Christ, like Socrates, like all redeemers, at the foot of his work. His work! Sublime achievement! over which humanity shall eternally shed its tears, and God his benedictions!

THE LAW, INDIVIDUAL LIBERTY, AND THE MOB SPIRIT.

JOHN WOODWARD.

From an address at the Chautauqua Assembly, August 15, 1903.

The common business and callings of life, the ordinary trades and pursuits which are innocent in themselves, and have been followed in all communities from time immemorial, must be free in this country to all alike upon the same terms. The right to pursue them without let or hinderance, except that which is applied to all persons of the same age, sex, and condition, is a distinguishing privilege of citizens of the United States, and an essential element of that freedom which they claim as their birthright.

This language was used to define the Constitutional limitations upon the Legislature, but it is equally applicable to the limitations which must, in a healthful condition of society, apply to individuals and associations of every character. The individual has a right to "pursue any lawful business or vocation in any manner not inconsistent with the equal rights of others," and this right is not increased or diminished by the fact that he becomes a member of a manufacturers' association, a labor organization, or any other voluntary society.

The manufacturer, whether he be an individual or a corporation, has a right to conduct his business, to control his property, in any manner not inconsistent with the equal rights of others. He has a right to employ such help as he chooses, being responsible to his other employees for any neglect in the choice of competent fellow-laborers, and society owes him the duty and the obligation of protecting him in this right against all unlawful efforts at coercion.

On the other hand the laborer, whether he belongs to an organization or is but a humble covenanter in the great system, has the absolute right to contract for his services with whomsoever he pleases, and the right to contract carries with it the right to determine the rate of compensation and all of the terms and conditions of the employment except such as may be regulated under the police powers of the State, and which enter, of necessity, into every contract.

Having these rights, these being the rights which we have mutually covenanted to protect, it is the duty of the State to insist that they shall not be encroached upon, either by individuals or organized bodies of individuals, under any pretext whatever. "The very idea of the power and the right of the people to establish government," says Washington, "presupposes the duty of every individual to obey the established government."

In what I have said I am not to be understood as condemning the labor organization as such, or the manufacturers' association, or any combination of individuals for their own ends. On the whole I am rather disposed to look upon the labor organization as the logical result of combination in capitalization, and upon both as the results of our economic system, and my criticism is rather of the inertness of the State and Nation, which has caused to be regarded with too much of indifference the tendency on the part of individuals, corporations, and associations to disregard the fundamental rights of man and to assume, in disregard of law, to adjust by force and intimidation their own controversies.

The rights of the laboring man are not safe when he may be coerced into refusing that employment which is essential to his "life, liberty, and the pursuit of happiness," and the welfare of the State and Nation demands that there shall be no compulsion exercised over the individual by any combination of men under any pretext, except such as is prescribed by the laws of the land. There is a broad field for organized effort in a perfectly legitimate and lawful way, among manufacturers, employers, and employees; and when any organization, no matter by what name it is called, goes beyond the limits marked by the law, it is the duty of good citizens, acting through the channels of the law, to assert themselves in the protection of the rights of those who are being encroached upon.

There is no other safety, there is no other way in which we can maintain that justice which "gives to each member of the community his due, without favor or affection."

INSIGHT AND FORESIGHT.

From the Outlook, June 27, 1903.

There are two forms of knowledge which the college can do but little to furnish, but which you must acquire if you are to succeed in life. Perhaps we should rather say, two forms of capacity: one is represented by the word Insight, the other by the word Foresight.

If you are to deal successfully with men, you must understand them. You must know their nature, and the motives which control them. If you are to live peaceably with them, you must know how to avoid needless friction. If you are to lead them, you must know how to win their confidence, esteem, respect. To do this you must enter into their lives, see things as they see them, get their point of view, be able to put yourself in their place. You must be able to do this not only for right-thinking, right-willing, and reasonable men; you must be able to do it for wrong-thinking, prejudiced, and unreasonable men, for with such men you will have to do in your life.

The other knowledge or capacity which you must acquire is Foresight. "There's a divinity that shapes our ends, rough-hew them how we will." We must understand what He is doing, to what end He is shaping our generation. We are like men upon the deck of an ocean steamer. We can walk forward or backward, or not walk at all; but we are borne on toward a distant point by forces which transcend our understanding, and which we can do little to direct. The currents which control our lives are almost wholly beyond our control, and we succeed in life only as we understand what those currents are and whither they are carrying us. We fail in life, however sagacious, strong, talented, and learned, if we set ourselves against those life-currents, endeavoring to thwart them, or if we live in ignorance of them, as though they did not exist. You must understand the currents of this age if you are to live successfully in it.

The individualism of the middle of the nineteenth century belongs to the past. Ruthless and unlimited competition is passing away. No human forces are strong enough to restore it. We are living in the age of combination and co-operation. The man who endeavors to prevent combination, whether of capital or of labor, swims against a resistless tide. He walks from the bow to the stern of a steamer which is steadily carrying him in the direction opposite to that in which he thinks he is walking. The wise leader of industry will neither ignore the competition of the past nor attempt to resist the tendency to coöperation and combination in the present. He will endeavor to see how, out of the competition of the past, to construct a combination and coöperation which will preserve the virtues and values of individualism, and secure also the virtues and values of a true, free, coöperative fellowship.

The tendency toward combination is as apparent in government as it is in industry. It is a part of the great movement toward universal brotherhood which can be guided, but cannot be thwarted. The separate and jealous provinces of Italy are united in one Italian kingdom. The hostile German States are united in one German Empire. Egypt, India, Australia, have become parts of the great British Empire. The frantic endeavor for the dissolution of the American commonwealth in the interests of political individualism failed. In lieu of it, the American flag floats not only over all the former American commonwealth, but, in spite of the protests of the timid, carries American sovereignty across the ocean to Hawaii and the Philippines. Commerce beckons American enterprise to enter the East, a thousand miles nearer our coast than to the British Isles, and opportunity demands of us a courage and a wisdom equal to the exigencies of the new day which dawns with the new century. To resist the tendency toward what men miscall imperialism is a hopeless task; to guide the tendency so that wherever the American flag carries with it American sovereignty, it shall also carry with it liberty, justice, and good will, is the problem which the God of nations calls on you to solve.

In religion the supreme and final authority has passed, for substantially all Protestant denominations, from the Church, and is passing, despite the hopeless resistance of many, from the Bible. The minister of the future must learn that the secret of authority is God in the individual conscience, and that the authority both of the Church and of the Bible is due to the fact that they have both interpreted that voice to human souls. He who would succeed in the religious development of his age must not live in the nineteenth century, still less in the sixteenth. He must live in the twentieth century, and must show men how to use both the Church and the Bible in interpreting that voice of God in the soul of man which is the secret of all authority — social, political, and religious.

You may not agree with this interpretation of the life-currents of this twentieth century. We briefly describe them, not for the purpose of making you see life as we see it, but for the purpose of inducing you to turn your faces toward the future and see for yourselves whither those life-currents are guiding you. The knowledge of the past will not give you success in the present, unless out of that past you learn lessons to guide you toward the future to which God is bringing the children of men. All that you have learned of history and literature, of science and of art,

in your college course will serve to enrich your life and
that of your fellow-men, will serve to give you real influence
over them and real leadership in your age, only as, to the
scholarship which the college has conferred upon you, you
add by your own individual study of life and men these
two vital qualities, Insight and Foresight — an understanding of men, and some comprehension of the future toward
which you must guide both them and yourself.

THE TRUE SPIRIT FOR INDEPENDENCE DAY.

YANCEY LEWIS.

An address delivered at the University of Texas, March 2, 1903.

We honor ourselves by celebrating this day. We prove
that we are not insensible to a heroic chapter in human history, nor lacking in gratitude to those by whose calm wisdom and supreme fortitude we have been blessed. But we do
not, we cannot, add aught of honor to those who made this
day memorable. High above our feeble tribute, their works
do honor them ; and their works endure. They endure in
the thrilling story which shall not only inspire us and our
successors after us, but shall strengthen the hearts of men
who, in distant times and under other skies, shall strike for
freedom. They endure in the wise policies by which the
administration of justice is simplified, the rights of woman-
hood enlarged, the rights of the family and the home safeguarded. They endure in this University, reared by courage
joined with wisdom, broad-based upon a people's will, consecrated to the education, without price, of all those, whether

low-born or powerful, who aspire to be free of the shackles of ignorance and to walk in the glorious light of knowledge. They endure in this great commonwealth, marked out by area, by climatic condition, by physical environment, and by the indwelling spirit of its people, for empire — in this huge leviathan among the States, not yet articulate, not yet having the unity of its highest purpose, nor wrought to its best hope, but destined ultimately, in my view, to speak with the strongest and most individual voice of all our States, and to be the most potent and controlling factor in our civilization.

If, then, we cannot honor the dead, how shall we make the observance of this day acceptable to them and serviceable to ourselves ?   The loud acclaim, the patriotic song, the studied oration, the deep-throated cannon's roar — these may be an empty pageantry, an idle hour's diversion.   How shall we make them vital and significant ?   Shall I tell you ?   By laying hold of the virtues of those who, on this day, declared their independence, by imbuing ourselves with their thoughts, by moving ourselves with their motives, by consecrating ourselves to their firm purposes and their high resolves, — by declaring this day *our* independence of all low motive or sordid desire or narrow view or ancient prejudice or hoary error ; by avowing this day that the ends we aim at shall be " our country's, our God's, and truth's."

Is there needed incentive to this obligation ?   Let me ask you : of those millions who during the ages have lived, labored, and died upon the earth, who have helped its progress or added to its freedom ?   I answer : those few, the immortals, whose names the world will not let die, who in some supreme juncture did, in the face of God and men, proclaim their independence. In geography, Columbus; in theology, Luther; in astronomy, Galileo; in government, Hampden and Washington; in religion, that strange divine Man of Galilee, gentlest and tenderest, most heroic and most independent of those who have walked upon earth. Is there need of this quality of independence now? Always, everywhere there is need of it. The earth's prayer well might be : " God, give us independent men." Never was there greater need of it than now. In our cities corruption enters into league with vice, takes with equal facility the name of either of the great parties, and boldly essays to rule. A race problem of appalling magnitude hangs over one section of our country, and beclouds the judgment of the other sections. Stupendous combinations of capital, vast armies of laborers, moved, marshalled, and directed like troops in the field, reverse old economic laws, present new and strange problems in our polity, and seem equally to threaten the rights and independence of the individual man. In our social life still goes on the world-old struggle between the material and the spiritual elements of our existence. Still is felt the invitation and the strong temptation, still is seen the fierce endeavor to put matter above mind, money above manhood, social position above social virtues, gain above knowledge, gold above God.

Let us, then, my friends, students of the University, on each recurring anniversary of this day, here in this University of Texas, whose site was dedicated by the founders of the republic, and whose muniments of title are such act of dedication, — the declaration of independence this day read, and the result at San Jacinto, — let us in this University strike hands with the ancient and goodly fellowship of Uni-

versity men of all time: with Stephen Langton, graduate of
the University of Paris, and leader in the movement which
wrung from John the Great Charter whose guaranties still
are vital in all our institutions, and whose phrases still ring
in the ears of freemen like the marching of armed men to
battle; with Hampden, son of Oxford, who gave his life to
save the liberties which the Great Charter granted; with
John Hancock and his majority of University men who
signed our American declaration of independence; with
Rusk and his majority of college men who put their names
to the declaration read to-day — let us strike hands with
them and pledge ourselves, as University men and Texans,
to love the truth and seek it, to learn the right and do it,
and, in all emergencies, however wealth may tempt or popular applause allure, to be sole rulers of our own free speech,
masters of our own untrammelled thoughts, captains of our
own unfettered souls.

In this spirit, to these ends, may we worthily celebrate
this day.

SOCIAL LIFE IN THE OLD SOUTH.

THOMAS NELSON PAGE.

Truly it was a charming life, the social life in the Old South.
There was a vast waste; but it was not loss. Every one had
food, every one had raiment, every one had peace. There
was not wealth in the base sense in which we know it and
strive for it and trample down others for it now. But there
was wealth in the good old sense in which the litany of our
fathers used it. There was weal. There was the best of

all wealth: there was content, and "a quiet mind is richer than a crown."

We have gained something by the change. The South under her new conditions will grow rich, will wax fat; nevertheless we have lost much. How much only those who knew it can estimate; to them it was inestimable.

That the social life of the Old South had its faults, I am far from denying. What civilization has not? But its virtues far outweighed them; its graces were never equalled. For all its faults, it was, I believe, the purest, sweetest life ever lived. It has been claimed that it was non-productive, that it fostered sterility. Only ignorance or folly could make the assertion. It largely contributed to produce this nation; it led its armies and its navies; it established this government so firmly that not even it could overthrow it; it opened up the great West; it added Louisiana and Texas, and more than trebled our territory; it Christianized the negro race in a little over two centuries, impressed upon it regard for order, and gave it the only civilization it has ever possessed since the dawn of history. It has maintained the supremacy of the Caucasian race, upon which all civilization seems now to depend. It produced a people whose heroic fight against the forces of the world has enriched the annals of the human race — a people whose fortitude in defeat has been even more splendid than their valor in war. It made men noble, gentle, and brave, and women tender, and pure, and true. It may have fallen short in material development in its narrower sense, but it abounded in spiritual development; it made the domestic virtues as common as light and air, and filled homes with purity and peace.

It has passed from the earth, but it has left its benignant

influence behind it to sweeten and sustain its children. The ivory palaces have been destroyed, but myrrh, aloes, and cassia still breathe amid their dismantled ruins.

THE NEGRO QUESTION.

THOMAS NELSON PAGE.

Professor James Bryce, in a recent paper on the negro question, arrives at the only reasonable conclusion : that the negro be let alone and the solution of the problem be left to the course of events. Friendship for the negro demands this. It has become the fashion of late for certain negro leaders to talk, in conventions held outside of the South, of fighting for their rights. For their own sake and that of their race, let them take it out in talking. A single outbreak would settle the question. To us of the South it appears that a proper race pride is one of the strongest securities of our nation. No people can become great without it. Without it no people can remain great. We propose to stand upon it.

Meantime, the negro is here, and something must be done. In the first place, let us have all the light that can be thrown on the subject. Form an organization to consider and deal with the subject, not in the spirit of narrowness or temper, but in the spirit of philosophic deliberation, such as becomes a great people discussing a great question which concerns not only their present but their future position among the nations. We shall then get at the right of the matter.

Let us do our utmost to eliminate from the question the complication of its political features. Get politics out of it, and the problem will be more than half solved. Senator Hampton stated not long ago, in a paper contributed by him, I think, to the *North American Review*, that, to get the negro out of politics, he would gladly give up the representation based on his vote. Could anything throw a stronger light on the apprehension with which the negro in politics is regarded at the South?

There never was any question more befogged with demagogism than that of manhood suffrage. Let us apply ourselves to securing some more reasonable and better basis for the suffrage. Let us establish such a proper qualification as a condition to the possession of the elective franchise as shall leave the ballot only to those who have intelligence enough to use it as an instrument to secure good government rather than to destroy it. In taking this step we have to plant ourselves on a broader principle than that of a race qualification. It is not merely the negro, it is ignorance and venality which we want to disfranchise. If we can disfranchise these, we need not fear the voter, whatever the color. At present it is not the negro who is disfranchised, but the white. We dare not divide.

Having limited him in a franchise which he has not in a generation learned to use, continue to teach him. It is from the educated negro, that is, the negro who is more enlightened than the general body of his race, that order must come. The ignorance, venality, and superstition of the average negro are dangerous to us. Education will divide them and will uplift them. They may learn in time that if they wish to rise, they must look to the essential qualities of good citizenship. In this way alone can the race, or any part of the race, look for ultimate salvation.

It has appeared to some that the South has not done its full duty by the negro. Perfection is, without doubt, a standard above humanity; but, at least, we of the South can say that we have done much for him; if we have not admitted him to social equality, it has been under an instinct stronger than reason, and in obedience to a law higher than is on the statute-books: the law of self-preservation. Slavery, whatever its demerits, was not in its time the unmitigated evil it is fancied to have been. Its time has passed. No power could compel the South to have it back. But to the negro it was salvation. It found him a savage and a cannibal, and in two hundred years gave seven millions of his race a civilization, the only civilization it has had since the dawn of history.

We have educated him; we have aided him; we have sustained him in all right directions. We are ready to continue our aid; but we will not be dominated by him. When we shall be, it is our settled conviction that we shall deserve the degradation into which we shall have sunk.

WEBSTER AS AN ORATOR.

HENRY CABOT LODGE.

Extract from an address delivered in Washington, January 18, 1900, on the occasion of the unveiling of a statue of Daniel Webster.

Eminent as a legislator, still more distinguished as a lawyer, Daniel Webster was supreme as an orator. There was no need for him to put pebbles in his mouth to cure stammering, or to rehearse his speeches on the seashore in conflict with the noise of the waves. He had from the hand of nature all the graces of person and presence, of voice and delivery, which the most exacting critic could demand, and these natural gifts were trained, enhanced, and perfected by years of practice in the senate, the court room, and before the people. In what he said he always had distinction — rarest of qualities — and he had also the great manner, just as Milton has it in verse. To lucid statement, to that simplicity in discussion which modern times demand for practical questions, to nervous force, he added, at his best, wealth of imagery, richness of diction, humor, and pathos, all combined with the power of soaring on easy wing to the loftiest flights of eloquence. Above all, he had that high and excellent seriousness which Aristotle sets down as one of the supreme virtues of poetry, and without which neither oratory nor poetry can attain supremacy.

It was not merely that as a statesman he saw the misery and degradation which would come from the breaking of the Union as well as the progressive disintegration which was sure to follow, but the very thought of it came home to him with the sharpness of a personal grief which was almost agonizing. When, in the seventh of March speech, he cried out, "What states are to secede? What is to remain American? What am I to be?" a political opponent said the tone of the last question made him shudder as if some dire calamity was at hand. The greatness of the United States filled his mind. He had not the length of days accorded to Lord Bathhurst, but the angel of dreams had unrolled to him the future, and the vision was ever before his eyes.

This passionate love of his country, this dream of her future, inspired his greatest efforts, were even the chief

cause at the end of his life of his readiness to make sacrifices of principle which would only have helped forward
what he dreaded most, but which he believed would save
that for which he cared most deeply.   In a period when
great forces were at work, which in their inevitable conflict
threatened the existence of the union of the states, Webster
stands out above all others as the champion, as the very
embodiment, of the national life and the national faith.
More than any other man of that time he called forth the
sentiment more potent than all reasonings which saved
the nation.   It was a great work, greatly done, with all the
resources of a powerful intellect and with an eloquence
rarely heard among men.   We may put aside all his other
achievements, all his other claims to remembrance, and in-
scribe alone upon the base of his statue the words uttered
in the senate, "Liberty and Union, now and forever, one
and inseparable."   That single sentence recalls all the
noble speeches which breathed only the greatness of the
country and the prophetic vision which looked with undaz-
zled gaze into a still greater future.   No other words are
wanted for a man who so represented and so expressed the
faith and hopes of a nation.   His statue needs no other
explanation so long as the nation he served and the Union
he loved shall last.

DEMOCRACY AND EDUCATION.

NICHOLAS MURRAY BUTLER.

From an address delivered before the National Educational Association, at Buffalo, N. Y., July 7, 1896.

The public education of a great democratic people has other aims to fulfil than the extension of scientific knowledge or the development of literary culture. It must prepare for intelligent citizenship. More than a century ago, Burke wrote that "the generality of people are fifty years, at least, behindhand in their politics. There are but very few who are capable of comparing and digesting what passes before their eyes at different times and occasions, so as to form the whole into a distinct system." This is the warning of one of the greatest of publicists, that a thoroughly instructed and competent public opinion on political matters is difficult to attain. Yet, unless we are to surrender the very principle on which democracy rests, we must struggle to attain it. Something may be accomplished by precept, something by direct instruction, much by example. The words "politics" and "politician" must be rescued from the low esteem into which they have fallen, and restored to their ancient and honorable meaning. It is safe to say that the framers of our Constitution never foresaw that the time would come when thousands of intelligent men and women would regard "politics" as beneath them, and when a cynical unwillingness to participate in the choice of persons and policies would develop among the people.

The difficulties of democracy are the opportunities of

education. If our education be sound, if it lay due emphasis on individual responsibility for social and political progress, if it counteract the anarchistic tendencies that grow out of selfishness and greed, if it promote a patriotism that reaches farther than militant jingoism and gunboats, then we may cease to have any doubts as to the perpetuity and integrity of our institutions. But I am profoundly convinced that the greatest educational need of our time, in higher and lower schools alike, is a fuller appreciation on the part of the teachers of what human institutions really mean and what tremendous moral issues and principles they involve. The ethics of individual life must be traced to its roots in the ethics of the social whole. The family, property, the common law, the state, and the church are all involved. These, and their products, taken together, constitute civilization and mark it off from barbarism. Inheritor of a glorious past, each generation is a trustee for posterity. To preserve, protect, and transmit its inheritance unimpaired is its highest duty. To accomplish this is not the task of a few, but the duty of all.

That democracy alone will be triumphant which has both intelligence and character. To develop them among the whole people is the task of education in a democracy. Not, then, by vainglorious boasting, not by self-satisfied indifference, not by selfish and indolent withdrawal from participation in the interests and government of the community, but rather by the enthusiasm, born of intense conviction, that finds the happiness of each in the good of all, will our educational ideals be satisfied and our free government be placed beyond the reach of the forces of dissolution and decay.

WEALTH AND DEMOCRACY.

LYMAN ABBOTT.

Despite the fact that wealth has never been so diffused, and the comforts wealth brings never so broadcast, as in America to-day, the thoughtful student of our national life must certainly recognize that the concentration of wealth is America's greatest peril, and a more equable distribution of wealth its greatest need. That cannot be counted either a Christian or a democratic state of society in which one per cent of the people own one-half of all the wealth, and the other half is very unequally distributed among the other ninety-nine per cent of owners, — in which there are a few millionnaires at one pole of society who cannot possibly spend their income, and many men and women at the other pole of society who have little or no income to spend. If Adam were created six thousand years ago, had lived until this time, and had succeeded in laying up one hundred dollars a day for every working day of the six thousand years of his life, he would not, without interest, have made as much money in six thousand years as the elder Cornelius Vanderbilt is said to have made in a lifetime. Jay Gould started in life with a mouse-trap; at the end of twenty-five years he unrolled certificates to the amount of a hundred million dollars. He made four million dollars on the average each year, that is to say, if we count three hundred days to the year, over thirteen thousand dollars a day; and the statisticians tell us that the average wages of unskilled labor in this country is less than one dollar a day, and of skilled working men not over four dollars a day as a maximum. In view of such inequalities as this, one need not be radical to believe with James Russell Lowell in "giving to the hands, not so large a share as to the brain, but a larger share than hitherto in the wealth they must combine to produce."

The economic problem of our age is how to secure the benefits of organization in producing wealth without incurring the evils of concentration in the possession and enjoyment of it. This is certainly not to be promoted by a blind distribution of the acquisitions of one class among the insatiable of another; nor by laws limiting the products of industry, or denying to the industrious the rewards of their toil. But there are other methods open to the consideration of the American student. He will remember that unjust systems of taxation have favored the few at the expense of the many, and he will question whether we have yet found a system of taxation absolutely just and equal. He will remember that in America, by our abolition of the right of primogeniture, we have limited the power of the "dead hand"; and he will question whether we may not still further limit the right of men whose wealth has been largely dependent upon the community, to control absolutely the disposition of that wealth in the community after they are dead. He will see that legislation has operated to discourage gambling and encourage productive industry, and he will ask whether further legislation in the same direction may not be both wise and desirable. He will remember that war has always cast its heaviest burdens on the poor, and he will question whether some more economical method of solving international difficulties cannot be discovered than the expensive and inefficient method of brute force. He will remember that, partly due to legislative influences, partly to influences purely social and industrial, the interest on capital has diminished and the wages of labor have increased, and he will ask himself the question whether this method of equalization of profits has reached its consummation. In short, he will believe that, as the effect of Christianity has been the diffusion of religious and intellectual life and of political power, so it has been, and is yet to be, the diffusion of wealth and its attendant comforts; and he will not be afraid to ask himself what can be done to promote still further that progress toward popular prosperity which Christ both promised and prophesied in His sermon at Nazareth.

For that this democratizing process is a distinctive characteristic of modern life can hardly be doubted. Art has never surpassed that of Phidias, but modern inventions put beauty into the homes of the humblest working-man. We still go back to Homer and to Aeschylus for literature, but the printing-press and the common school put the best literature within the reach of the poorer people. Modern education is universal. Temples do not outshine those of Jerusalem, Ephesus, Rome, but there is a church in every village. There are no saints who in spiritual vision and consecrated life transcend the Apostle Paul, but into the slums of every modern city apostles with the Pauline spirit are carrying the message of God's love for man and of man's love for his fellow-men. The process begun in Galilee, however, is not yet completed, and will not be until political economy learns and teaches the doctrine of distribution as well as of accumulation; until fools cease to hoard and wise men learn to scatter; until every " boss " is dismissed, and every ring broken; until our systems of public education recognize the truth that to think is more than to know, and to be is more than to think; until, in the words of the ancient prophet, "every valley is filled, and every mountain is brought low."

GOVERNMENT BY PUBLIC OPINION.

ARTHUR TWINING HADLEY.

Extract from an address delivered at the Charter Day Exercises of the University of California, March 23, 1901.

The question is often asked, what constitutes the essential mark of a gentleman, as distinct from the accidents of birth and of clothes, of manners and of speech. I believe it is to be found in the readiness to accept trusts, even when they are personally disadvantageous, — the readiness to subordinate a man's own convenience and desires to a social code. The code may be a good one or a bad one; but it is an authority which the gentleman accepts of his own free will, without waiting for any one to compel him to accept it. To the extent that he does this, he not only proves himself a gentleman, but proves himself capable of self-government. In this sense I believe that the great body of the American people are gentlemen; and that this is the best guarantee for the permanence of our system of self-government amid the increasing difficulties with which it has to deal. There is much which is as yet defective in our commercial and political code of honor. But the fundamental fault is in the code and not in the man; and therefore the task of the reformer is no insuperable one.

The thing that makes democracy practicable is a willingness, on the part of the mass of the people, to submit to self-imposed authority without waiting for the policeman to enforce it. The cause of democracy was the distribution of fighting power, which formerly had been confined to one class. The possibility of maintaining democracy is due to the fact that the readiness to accept self-imposed burdens has gone hand in hand with the distribution of power. The danger of democracy lies in the adoption of a false code of honor, which tolerates and approves the pursuit of self-interest in lines where it must prove ultimately destructive to the community. If our men of influence can see these dangers in time to submit to self-imposed restrictions, they can preserve their freedom from legislative interference, and our republic can remain as it now is, a self-governing body. If they do not see it in time, the demands for the extension of legislative machinery and police activity will so far restrict our personal liberty that democratic freedom will exist only in name, and we shall have a social order where the form of an occasional election is but a decent veil to disguise struggles for the tyranny of one class over another.

It is for the young men who are coming on the field of political life to-day to guard against this danger. Our college students have lived in communities which have their historic traditions and their collective aspirations; each of which is in a true sense a body politic, with its public spirit and its public sentiment. It is for them to carry into the larger world of business and of legislation the spirit which will subordinate personal convenience to collective honor. Let them cease to appeal exclusively to self-interest, either in their own judgment or in the judgment of others. For a political leader who has not only fixed standards of right, but a belief in the capacity of the people to accept those standards, the times are always ready. Calhoun and Clay and Webster and Lincoln differed in their judgments and in their conclusions. But it was characteristic of them all that they made their final appeal, not to the narrow interests of any class, but to what they believed to be broad principles of public opinion and public morality. It was in the spirit of these men that our republic gained its growth during the century that is past; it is for us, their sons, to see that the same spirit is applied to the yet larger problems of the century which is to come.

THE LAW OF SERVICE.

LYMAN ABBOTT.

There are a variety of ways in which men add to the world's wealth, — that is, to its life, physical, intellectual, moral. In the natural order, the first thing is to get out of the earth what the earth contains for the service of man. This is the work of the agriculturist, the miner, the lumberman. These men are making available to the community the reservoired resources of the globe. But one cannot advantageously eat raw wheat, nor live in trees, nor use iron (in the ore) for tools, nor comfortably wear the skins of animals. The wheat must be turned into bread, the trees builded into houses, the iron fashioned into tools, the wool spun and woven into garments. Thus the second thing is to turn what the earth gives us into forms useful for our service. This is a mechanic art. In one region there is plenty of food, in another none; in one, forest, in another timberless plains and valleys; in one the iron mine, in another the millstream or the coal which furnishes power for the factory. The food must be transported from the Western prairie to the Eastern city; the timber from the Michigan forest to the Illinois farm; the iron or copper from the shores of Lake Superior to the furnaces of Pennsylvania. Thus comes into play the third great service to the community,— transportation. China and India suffer great famines,— unknown in America,—chiefly because they are not equipped with great railroad corporations to carry supplies from the regions where food is abundant to the regions which are famine-stricken. When these supplies are brought to the communities who need them, there must be individuals to carry this work of distribution further. These are called middlemen. It is popular in certain quarters to condemn the middlemen, but they are essential to public well-being. As modern waterworks gather the water into reservoirs, send it by means of great mains throughout the city, from which again it is distributed in smaller and still smaller pipes, until it reaches the rooms in the private houses, where it can be drawn by opening a faucet, so commerce takes nature's supplies, carries them to great centres of population, where retail trade takes them up, distributing them to individual households. The middleman is the faucet, without which the water would never be available in the home.

We have, however, other needs than material ones. Men will sicken, there must be skilled physicians; men will not understand their right relations to one another, there must be lawyers to counsel them; there are criminals, and there must be governors, soldiers, policemen, to protect. There must be teachers to instruct, preachers and poets to inspire, artists and authors and musicians to minister to the æsthetic and literary taste. There will be homes, and there must be wives and mothers who are not turning the spinning-wheel, nor driving the loom, nor ploughing the field, nor adding to the material wealth by their industry, but who are adding to spiritual wealth by their patience, their fidelity, and their love. In all this work, hand and brain must coöperate. Labor is not all hand labor. An American humorist has said, with great truth, " In the sweat of thy brow shalt thou eat bread, but some men sweat outside and some men inside." The brain has need of the hand, and the hand of the brain. Both are entitled to their share of the world's products, but this one fundamental truth remains : the world has just so much as we put into it; no more. If we do not by our consecrated use of hand, or head, or heart, by our personal activity or our wise direction of the activity of others, by our serving or by our suffering, endeavor to add to the world's wealth — material, intellectual, or spiritual — at least as much as we have taken out of it, we belong in the category of the beggars, the thieves, and the gamblers.

The first principle, then, is respect for labor and respect for each other's labor; respect by the man who works with his brain for the man who works with his hand, and respect by the man who works with his hand for the man who works with his brain — mutual respect. When we have thoroughly learned this one fundamental principle, that to destroy is not honorable and to produce is, that the glory of the nation lies in its production, that the glory of life lies in adding to the wealth of life — its material, its intellectual, its spiritual wealth, — we shall have learned one great underlying lesson. Until we have learned this, all other learning is in vain, for this is the foundation. The greatest of all is the servant of all. We believe this in the church: the minister is the servant of the congregation. We believe it in politics: the President is the servant of the people. We shall not get to the Christian basis of industry until we come to recognize in industry, also, that there is no independence, and that the greatest, and the richest, and the strongest, is great only as he is the servant of the weak and poor.

JOHN MARSHALL.

HENRY CABOT LODGE.

From an address delivered before the Bar Associations of Illinois and Chicago, February 4, 1901.

The monumental decisions of Chief Justice Marshall, handed down during thirty-five years of judicial life, are more than a monument of legal reasoning, more than a masterly exposition of the Constitution, for they embody the well-considered policy of a great statesman. They are the work of a man who saw that the future of the United States hinged upon the one question whether the national should prevail over the separatist principle, whether the nation was to be predominant over the states — whether, indeed, there was to be a nation at all. Through all the issues which rose and fell during these thirty-five years, through all the excitements of the passing day, through Louisiana acquisitions and the relations with France and England, through embargoes and war and Missouri compromises, and all the bitter, absorbing passions which they aroused, the Chief Justice in his court went steadily forward dealing with that one underlying question beside which all others were insignificant. Slowly but surely he did his work. He made men understand that a tribunal existed before which states could be forced to plead, by which state laws could be annulled, and which was created by the Constitution. He took the dry clauses of that Constitution and breathed into them the breath of life. Knowing well the instinct of human nature to magnify its own possessions, — an instinct more potent than party feeling, — he had pointed out and developed for presidents and congresses the powers given them by the Constitution from which they derived their own existence. Whether these presidents and congresses were Federalist or Democratic, they were all human and would be certain, therefore, to use sooner or later the powers disclosed to them. That which Hamilton, in the bitterness of defeat, had called "a frail and worthless fabric," Marshall converted into a mighty instrument of government. The Constitution, which began as an agreement between conflicting states, Marshall, continuing the work of Washington and Hamilton, transformed into a charter of national life. When his own life closed his work was done — a nation had been made. Before he died he heard this great fact declared with unrivalled eloquence by Webster. It was reserved to another generation to put Marshall's work to the last and awful test of war, and to behold it come forth from that dark ordeal, triumphant and supreme.

What of the man who did all this? The statesman we know, the great lawyer, the profound jurist, the original thinker, the unrivalled reasoner. All this is there in his decisions and in his public life, carved deep in the history of the times. But of the man himself we know little; in proportion to his greatness and the part he played, we know nothing. He was a silent man, doing his great work in the world and saying nothing of himself, to a degree quite unknown to any of the heroes of Carlyle, who preached the doctrine of silence so strenuously in many volumes. Marshall seems to have destroyed all his own papers; certainly none of consequence are known to exist now. He wrote but few letters, if we may judge from the voluminous collection of the time, where, if we except those addressed to Judge Story, lately published, he is less represented than any of the other leaders of that period. Brief memories by some of his contemporaries, scattered letters, stray recollections and fugitive descriptions, are all that we have to help us to see and know the man John Marshall. Yet his personality is so strong that from these fragments and from the study of his public life it stands forth to all who look with understanding and sympathy. A great intellect; a clear sight which was never dimmed, but which always recognized facts and scorned delusions; a powerful will; a courage, moral, mental, and physical, which nothing could daunt, — all these things lie upon the surface. Deeper down we discern a directness of mind, a purity and strength of character, a kind heart, an abundant humor, and a simplicity and modesty which move our admiration as beyond the bounds of eulogy. He was a very great man. The proofs of his greatness lie all about us, in our history, our law, our constitutional development, our public thought. But there is one witness to his greatness of soul which seems to me to outweigh all the others. He had been a soldier and lawyer and statesman; he had been an envoy to France, a member of Congress, Secretary of State, and Chief Justice. He did

a great work, and no one knew better than he how great i
had been. Then when he came to die he wrote his own
epitaph, and all he asked to have recorded was his name,
the date of his birth, the date of his marriage, and the date
of his death. What a noble pride and what a fine simplicity
are there! In the presence of such a spirit, at the close of
such a life, almost anything that can be said would seem
tawdry and unworthy. His devoted friend, Judge Story,
wished to have inscribed upon Marshall's tomb the words,
"Expounder of the Constitution." Even this is something
too much and also far too little. He is one of that small
group of men who have founded states. He is a nation-
maker, a state-builder. His monument is in the history of
the United States, and his name is written upon the Constitution of his country.

EVENTS ARE TEMPORAL, PRINCIPLES ETERNAL.

NICHOLAS MURRAY BUTLER.

*The Introduction to a speech at the Fortieth Annual Convocation of
the University of the State of New York, June 30, 1902.*

It was my good fortune to hear one of General Garfield's
most eloquent speeches. From the gallery of a great hall I
looked down upon a scene where ambition, envy, and patriotism were all struggling for expression in the national convention of a powerful political party. A candidate for
President of the United States was to be chosen. The walls
had trembled at the mighty cheers that thousands of strong,
eager men had given for the leaders of their choice. Finally,
amid perfect silence, General Garfield rose in his place

among the representatives of Ohio and made his way to the platform to put before the convention the name of the man whom he preferred above all others for President of the United States. He had been greatly moved by the tempest of cheering and applause which had greeted two of the names already in nomination, and he sought to lead the convention away from the passionate feeling of the moment to a more sober and substantial standard of judgment. With solemnity and deliberation, General Garfield opened his speech with these sentences : —

"I have witnessed the extraordinary scenes of this convention with deep solicitude. Nothing touches my heart more quickly than a tribute of honor to a great and noble character; but as I sat in my seat and witnessed this demonstration, this assemblage seemed to me a human ocean in tempest. I have seen the sea lashed into fury and tossed into spray, and its grandeur moves the soul of the dullest man; but I remember that it is not the billows, but the calm level of the sea, from which all heights and depths are measured.

"When the storm has passed and the hour of calm settles on the ocean, when the sunlight bathes its peaceful surface, then the astronomer and surveyor take the level from which they measure all terrestrial heights and depths.

"Not here, in this brilliant circle where one hundred and fifty thousand men and women are gathered, is the destiny of the republic to be decreed for the next four years, — not here, where I see the enthusiastic faces of seven hundred and fifty-six delegates, waiting to cast their lots into the urn and determine the choice of the republic, — but by four millions of Republican firesides, where the thoughtful voters, with wives and children about them, with the calm thoughts inspired by love of home and country, with the history of the past, the hopes of the future, and reverence for the great men who have adorned and blessed our nation in days gone by, burning in their hearts — there God prepares the verdict which will determine the wisdom of our work to-night."

Often in listening to debates and discussions of matters far removed from things political, this counsel of Garfield's has recurred to me. It seems to be so easy, in education as elsewhere, to yield to the pressure of momentary feeling or temporary expediency and to lose sight of the deep, underlying principles which should, and in the long run must, control our action and our policies, that we need constant reminders of what those principles are.

THE PURITANS AND TWENTIETH CENTURY PROBLEMS.

ARTHUR TWINING HADLEY.

From an address delivered before the New England Society of New York City, December 22, 1900.

By nine persons out of ten, the Puritans of the seventeenth century are remembered chiefly for the pattern of their clothes or the phraseology of their creeds; and even the tenth man, who really goes below the surface, often lays wrong emphasis on the different parts of their activity, and fails to understand the true reason of their power. He thinks of the Puritan not so much for what he did as for what he refused to do and forbade others to do; as one who held himself aloof from the joys of life and apart from the sympathies of humanity.

Not in such restrictions and refusals was the strength of the Puritan character founded. Not by any such negative virtue did he conquer the world. The true Puritan was intensely human — a man who " ate when he was hungry and drank when he was thirsty; loved his friends and hated his enemies." If he submitted to self-imposed hardships, and practised abstention where others allowed themselves latitude, it was not because he had less range of interest than his fellows, but because he had more range. He did these things as a means to an end. His thoughts went beyond the limits of the single day or the single island. He was a man who considered power as more than possession, principles as better than acquirements, public duty as paramount to personal allegiance. He regarded himself as part of a universe under God's government. For the joy of taking his place in that government, he steeled himself to a temper which spared not his own body nor that of others. His life, with all its powers, was held in trust. To the fulfilment of this trust he subordinated all considerations of personal pleasure.

Men are always divided more or less clearly into two types, — those who recognize this character of life as a trust, and those who fail to recognize it. It was because England had men of the former type that her subsequent progress as a free nation has been realized. It was the Puritan who, by subjecting his power and his love of life to self-imposed restraints, made freedom possible in two hemispheres.

Once more we are to come to a similar parting of the ways. The close of the nineteenth century has witnessed an expansion of the geographical boundaries of men's interests comparable only to that which came three hundred years earlier, in the days of Queen Elizabeth. It is for the next generation to decide how these new fields shall be occupied. Shall it be to gratify ambition, commercial and political ? or shall it be to exercise a trust which has been given us for the advancement of the human race? Shall we enter upon our new possessions in the spirit of the adventurer, or in the spirit of the Puritan ? The conflict between these two views will be the really important issue in the complex maze of international relations during the half century which is to come. The outcome of this conflict is likely to determine the course of the world's history for ages thereafter.

Now, it is not in international politics and in problems of colonization alone that this issue is arising between those who regard the world as a field for pleasure and those who regard it as a place for the exercise of a trust. The development of modern industry has placed the alternative even more sharply before us in the ordering of our life at home. The day is past when the automatic action of self-interest could be trusted to regulate prices, or when a few simple principles of commercial law, if properly applied, secured the exercise of justice in matters of trade. The growth of large industries and of large fortunes enables those who use them rightly to do the public much better service than was possible in ages previous. It also permits those who use them wrongly to render the public correspondingly greater injury. No system of legislation is likely to meet this difficulty. The outcome depends on the character of the people. Is our business to be dominated by the spirit of the adventurer, or by the spirit of the Puritan? Shall we regard wealth as a means of enjoyment and commercial power, as a plaything to be used in the game of personal ambition? or shall we treat the fortunes which come into our hands as a trust to be exercised for the benefit of the people, rigidly abstaining from its abuse ourselves, and unsparingly refusing to associate with others who abuse it? No American has a right to claim a share in the glory of the Pilgrim Fathers if he has any doubt concerning his answer. Let us throw ourselves, heart and soul, on that side of the industrial question which proves us worthy of Puritan ancestry, — the side which regards wealth as a trust, to be used in behalf of the whole people and in the furtherance of the purposes of God's government.

THE SYMMETRY OF LIFE.

PHILLIPS BROOKS.

Extract from an Address to Young Men.

There are three directions or dimensions of human life to which we may fitly give these three names, Length and Breadth and Height. The Length of a life, in this meaning of it, is, of course, not its duration. It is the rather the reaching on and out of a man, in the line of activity and thought and self-development, which is indicated and prophesied by the character which is natural within him, by the special ambitions which spring up out of his special powers. It is the push of a life forward to its own personal ends and ambitions. The Breadth of a life, on the other hand, is its outreach laterally, if we may say so. It is the constantly diffusive tendency which is always drawing a man outward into sympathy with other men. And the Height of a life is its upward reach towards God; its sense of childhood; its consciousness of a Divine Life over it with which it tries to live in love, communion and obedience. These are the three dimensions of a life, — its length and breadth and height, — without the due development of all of which no life becomes complete. The life which has only length, only intensity of ambition, is narrow. The life that has length and breadth, intense ambition and broad humanity, is thin; it is like a great, flat plain, of which one wearies, and which sooner or later wearies of itself. The life which to its length and breadth adds height, which to its personal ambition and sympathy with men, adds the love and obedience of God, completes itself into the cube of the eternal city and is the life complete.

Think for a moment of the life of the great apostle, the manly, many-sided Paul. "I press toward the mark for the prize of my high calling," he writes to the Philippians. That is the length of life for him. "I will gladly spend and be spent for you," he writes to the Corinthians. There is the breadth of life for him. "God hath raised us up and made us sit together in heavenly places in Christ Jesus," he writes to the Ephesians. There is the height of life for him. You can add nothing to these three dimensions when you try to account to yourself for the impression of completeness which comes to you out of his simple, lofty story.

We need not stop with him. Look at the Lord of Paul. See how in Christ the same symmetrical manhood shines yet more complete. See what intense ambition to complete

His work, what tender sympathy with every struggling brother by His side, and at the same time what a perpetual dependence on His Father, is in Him. "For this cause came I into the world." "For their sakes I sanctify myself." "Now, O Father, glorify Thou me." Leave either of those out and you have not the perfect Christ, not the entire symmetry of manhood.

If we try to gather into shape some picture of what the perfect man of heaven is to be, still we must keep the symmetry of these his three dimensions. It must be that forever before each glorified spirit in the other life there shall be set one goal of peculiar ambition, his goal, after which he is peculiarly to strive, the struggle after which is to make his eternal life to be forever different from every other among all the hosts of heaven. And yet it must be that as each soul strives towards his own attainment he shall be knit forever into closer and closer union with all the other countless souls which are striving after theirs. And the inspiring power of it all, the source of all the energy and all the love, must then be clear beyond all doubt; the ceaseless flood of light forever pouring forth from the self-living God to fill and feed the open lives of His redeemed who lived by him. There is the symmetry of manhood perfect. There, in redeemed and glorified human nature, is the true heavenly Jerusalem.

I hope that we are all striving and praying now that we may come to some such symmetrical completeness. This is the glory of a young man's life. Do not dare to live without some clear intention toward which your living shall be bent. Mean to do something with all your might. Do not add act to act and day to day in perfect thoughtlessness, never asking yourself whither the growing line is leading. But at the same time do not dare to be so absorbed in your own life, so wrapped up in listening to the sound of your own hurrying heels, that all this vast pathetic music, made up of the mingled joy and sorrow of your fellow-men, shall not find out your heart and claim it and make you rejoice to give yourself for them. And yet, all the while, keep the upward windows open. Do not dare to think that a child of God can worthily work out his career or worthily serve God's other children unless he does both in the love and fear of God their Father. Be sure that ambition and charity will both grow mean unless they are both inspired and exalted by religion. Energy, love, and faith, those make the perfect man. And Christ, who is the perfectness of all of them, gives them all three to any young man who, at the very outset of his life, gives up himself to Him.

INDEX.

255

The Academy Series of English Classics.

THE works selected for this series are such as have gained a conspicuous and enduring place in literature ; nothing is admitted either trivial in character or ephemeral in interest. Each volume is edited by a teacher of reputation, whose name is a guaranty of sound and judicious annotation. It is the aim of the Notes to furnish assistance only where it is absolutely needed, and, in general, to permit the author to be his own interpreter.

All the essays and speeches in the series (excepting Webster's Reply to Hayne) are printed without abridgment. The Plays of Shakespeare are expurgated only where necessary for school use.

Addison. *De Coverley Papers.* Edited by Samuel Thurber. Cloth, 35 cents.

Arnold. *Essays in Criticism.* Edited by Susan S. Sheridan. Cloth, 25 cents.
Rugby Chapel. Edited by L. D. Syle. (In *Four English Poems.* Cloth, 25 cents.)
Sohrab and Rustum. Edited by George A. Watrous. (In *Three Narrative Poems.* Cloth, 30 cents.)

Burke. *Conciliation with the Colonies.* Edited by C. B. Bradley. Cloth, 30 cents.

Burns. *Selections.* Edited by Lois G. Hufford. Cloth, 35 cents.

Byron. *The Prisoner of Chillon.* Edited by L. D. Syle. (In *Four English Poems.* Cloth, 25 cents.)

Carlyle. *Essay on Burns.* Edited by H. W. Boynton. Cloth, 25 cents.
Essay on Boswell's Johnson. Edited by H. W. Boynton. Boards, 20 cents.

Coleridge. *The Ancient Mariner.* Edited by George A. Watrous. (In *Three Narrative Poems.* Cloth, 30 cents.)

Cowper. *John Gilpin's Ride.* Edited by L. D. Syle. (In *Four English Poems.* Cloth, 25 cents.)

George Eliot. *Silas Marner.* Edited by W. Patterson Atkinson. Cloth, 30 cents.

Emerson. *Select Essays and Poems.* Edited by Eva March Tappan. Cloth, 30 cents.

Goldsmith. *The Vicar of Wakefield.* Edited by R. Adelaide Witham. Cloth, 40 cents.
The Traveller and *The Deserted Village.* Edited by George A. Watrous. (In *Selected Poems.* Cloth, 30 cents.)

Academy Series of English Classics. (*Continued*)

Gray. *Elegy Written in a Country Churchyard* and *The Progress of Poesy.* Edited by G. A. Watrous. (In *Selected Poems.* Cloth, 30 cents.)

Irving. *Life of Goldsmith.* Edited by R. Adelaide Witham. Cloth, 40 cents.

Selections from the Sketch Book. Edited by Elmer E. Wentworth. Cloth, 35 cents.

Lowell. *Selections. The Vision of Sir Launfal and other Poems.* Edited by Dr. F. R. Lane. Cloth, 25 cents.

Macaulay. Edited by Samuel Thurber.

Essay on Addison ; Clive ; Hastings ; Milton. Cloth, each, 25 cents.

Essay on Chatham ; Johnson. Boards, each, 20 cents.

Essays on Milton and Addison. One volume, cloth, 35 cents.

Milton. *Paradise Lost, Books I. and II.* Edited by Henry W. Boynton. Cloth, 30 cents.

Minor Poems. Edited by Samuel Thurber. Cloth, 30 cents.

Pope. *The Rape of the Lock.* Edited by L. D. Syle. (In *Four English Poems.* Cloth, 25 cents.)

An Essay on Criticism. Edited by George A. Watrous. (In *Selected Poems.* Cloth, 30 cents.)

Scott. *The Lady of the Lake.* Edited by G. B. Aiton. Cloth, 30 cents.

Marmion. Edited by Mary E. Adams. Cloth, 30 cents.

Shakespeare. Edited by Samuel Thurber.

As You Like It ; Julius Cæsar ; Merchant of Venice ; Macbeth. Cloth, each, 30 cents.

The Tempest. Boards, 20 cents ; cloth, 30 cents.

Hamlet (with Pearson's *Questions on Hamlet*). Cloth, 35 cents.

Tennyson. *Enoch Arden.* Edited by George A. Watrous. (In *Three Narrative Poems.* Cloth, 30 cents.)

Idylls of the King : Selections. Edited by H. W. Boynton. Cloth, 30 cents.

Webster. *Reply to Hayne.* Edited by C. B. Bradley. Cloth, 25 cents.

Four English Poems : *The Rape of the Lock, John Gilpin's Ride, The Prisoner of Chillon,* and *Rugby Chapel.* Edited by L. D. Syle. Cloth, 25 cents.

Three Narrative Poems : *The Ancient Mariner, Sohrab and Rustum,* and *Enoch Arden.* Edited by G. A. Watrous. Cloth, 30 cents.

Selected Poems from Pope, Gray, and Goldsmith. Edited by George A. Watrous. Cloth, 30 cents.

Paragraph-Writing

By Professors F. N. SCOTT, of the University of Michigan, and J. V. DENNEY, of Ohio State University. 12mo, cloth, 304 pages. Price, $1.00.

THIS is a text-book in Composition for the Freshman year of college. The principles embodied in the work were developed and put into practice by its authors at the University of Michigan. Its aim is to make the paragraph the basis of a method of composition, and to present all the important facts of rhetoric in their application to it.

The book is in three parts: in Part I the nature and laws of the paragraph are presented; the isolated paragraph, its structure and function, are discussed; and considerable space is devoted to related paragraphs, — that is, those which are combined into essays. Part II is a chapter on the theory of the paragraph intended for teachers and advanced students. In Part III will be found copious material for classroom work, — selected paragraphs, suggestions to teachers, lists of subjects for compositions (about two thousand in all), and helpful references of many kinds. Appendix H treats of the Rhetoric of the Paragraph.

The College Literature Review

By Professor F. E. BRYANT, of the University of Kansas. Price, each, 10 cents; per dozen, $1.00.

THIS is a blank book for the use of college classes in literature and composition. On the covers are printed Hints on Reading and on the Preparation of the Review; and also questions suggesting various methods of treatment.

Questions on Shakespeare: Hamlet

By Professor P. H. PEARSON, of Bethany College, Kansas. 15 cents.

THIS book contains a number of carefully chosen questions on the interpretation of Hamlet, designed either for examination purposes or to aid the pupil to read the play thoughtfully and intelligently.

4

The Drama: Its Law and its Technique

By ELISABETH WOODBRIDGE, Ph.D. 12mo, cloth, 198 pages. Price, 80 cents.

THE object of this book is to present a manual for use in college courses on the drama, which shall stand the test of actual classroom use. It is successful in avoiding the principal defects of previous short treatises on the subject, which have been made up too completely of theories on the art, or have occupied themselves too exclusively with practical stage-craft.

The chapters are : —

LAW	TECHNIQUE
I. Poetic Truth.	I. The Two Types of Drama.
II. Dramatic Unity.	II. The Logical Divisions of the Action.
III. Seriousness, ΣΠΟΥΔΗ.	III. The Mechanical Division of the Drama.
IV. The Nature and Sources of Tragic Effect.	IV–VI. Character-Treatment and Plot in Comedy.
V. The Nature and Sources of Comic Effect.	

Its broader foundations are laid in Freytag's Technik des Dramas, but it follows Freytag's footsteps only where it is unavoidable to any one venturing on the ground at all. The discussion itself is an original treatment on lines adapted to give the student a real knowledge and a permanent appreciation of the structure of the drama.

Selections from Carlyle

Edited by H. W. BOYNTON. 12mo, cloth, 288 pages. Price, 75 cents.

THIS volume includes material for the elementary study of Carlyle in his earliest and most fruitful period. It contains the Essays on Burns, on History, on Boswell's Life of Johnson, and selections from Heroes and Hero-Worship (the Introduction ; the Hero as Poet — Dante, Shakespeare ; and the Hero as Man of Letters — Johnson, Rousseau, Burns).

De Quincey's Essays on Style, Rhetoric, and Language

Edited by Professor FRED N. SCOTT, University of Michigan. 12mo, 275 pages. Price, 60 cents.

THE essays selected are those which deal directly with the theory of literature. The appendix contains such passages from De Quincey's other writings as will be of most assistance to the student.

Principles of Success in Literature

By GEORGE HENRY LEWES. Edited with Introduction and Notes by Professor FRED N. SCOTT. 12mo, 163 pages. Price, 50 cents.

THE object of reprinting this admirable little treatise on literature is to make it available for classes in rhetoric and literary criticism. Scarcely any other work will be found so thoroughly sound in principles, and so suggestive and inspiring.

The value of the present edition is greatly increased by the excellent introduction by Professor Scott, and by a full index.

Spencer's Philosophy of Style and Wright's Essay on Style

Edited by Professor FRED N. SCOTT, of the University of Michigan. 12mo, 92 pages. Price, 45 cents.

THE plan has been followed of providing a biographical and critical introduction, an index, and a few notes. In the belief that the Philosophy of Style can best be understood in connection with the Spencerian philosophy as a whole, the Introduction has been made largely bibliographical. There are Appendices giving a criticism of Spencer's theory of the effect of rhythmical structure from Gurney's Power of Sound, and an extract from Spencer's First Principles touching the evolution of literature.

10

Orations and Arguments

Edited by Professor C. B. BRADLEY, University of California. 12mo, cloth, 385 pages. Price, $1.00.

The following speeches are contained in the book: —

BURKE:
On Conciliation with the Colonies, and Speech before the Electors at Bristol.

CHATHAM:
On American Affairs.

ERSKINE:
In the Stockdale Case.

LINCOLN:
The Gettysburg Address.

WEBSTER:
The Reply to Hayne.

MACAULAY:
On the Reform Bill of 1832.

CALHOUN:
On the Slavery Question.

SEWARD:
On the Irrepressible Conflict.

IN making this selection, the test applied to each speech was that it should be in itself memorable, attaining its distinction through the essential qualities of nobility and force of ideas, and that it should be, in topic, so related to the great thoughts, memories, or problems of our own time as to have for us still an inherent and vital interest.

The speeches thus chosen have been printed from the best available texts, without change, save that the spelling has been made uniform throughout, and that three of the speeches — those of Webster, Calhoun, and Seward — have been shortened somewhat by the omission of matters of merely temporal or local interest. The omitted portions have been summarized for the reader, whenever they bear upon the main argument.

The Notes aim to furnish the reader with whatever help is necessary to the proper appreciation of the speeches; to avoid bewildering him with mere subtleties and display of erudition; and to encourage in him habits of self-help and familiarity with sources of information.

A special feature of this part of the work is a sketch of the English Constitution and Government, intended as a general introduction to the English speeches.

The collection includes material enough to permit of a varied selection for the use of successive classes in the schools.

From Milton to Tennyson

Masterpieces of English Poetry. Edited by L. Du Pont Syle. 12mo, cloth, 480 pages. Price, $1.00.

IN this work the editor has endeavored to bring together within the compass of a moderate-sized volume as much narrative, descriptive, and lyric verse as a student may reasonably be required to read critically for entrance to college. From the nineteen poets represented, only such masterpieces have been selected as are within the range of the understanding and the sympathy of the high school student. Each masterpiece is given complete, except for pedagogical reasons in the cases of Thomson, Cowper, Byron, and Browning. Exigencies of space have compelled the editor reluctantly to omit Scott from this volume. The copyright laws, of course, exclude American poets from the scope of this work.

The following poets are represented : —

MILTON	L'Allegro, Il Penseroso, Lycidas, and a Selection from the Sonnets.
DRYDEN	Epistle to Congreve, Alexander's Feast, Character of a Good Parson.
POPE	Epistles to Mr. Jervas, to Lord Burlington, and to Augustus.
THOMSON	Winter.
JOHNSON	Vanity of Human Wishes.
GRAY	Elegy Written in a Country Churchyard, and The Bard.
GOLDSMITH	Deserted Village.
COWPER	Winter Morning Walk.
BURNS	Cotter's Saturday Night, Tam O'Shanter, and a Selection from the Songs.
COLERIDGE	Ancient Mariner.
BYRON	Isles of Greece, and Selections from Childe Harold, Manfred, and the Hebrew Melodies.
KEATS	Eve of St. Agnes, Ode to a Nightingale, Sonnet on Chapman's Homer.
SHELLEY	Euganean Hills, The Cloud, The Skylark, and the Two Sonnets on the Nile.
WORDSWORTH	Laodamia, The Highland Girl, Tintern Abbey, The Cuckoo, The Ode to a Skylark, The Milton Sonnet, The Ode to Duty, and the Ode on the Intimations of Immortality.
MACAULAY	Horatius.
CLOUGH	Two Ships, the Prologue to the Mari Magno, and the Lawyer's First Tale.
ARNOLD	The Scholar-Gypsy and the Forsaken Merman.
BROWNING	Transcript from Euripides (Balaustion's Adventure).
TENNYSON	Œnone, Morte D'Arthur, The Miller's Daughter, and a Selection from the Songs.

Articulation ⎱ 10   Grade
Enunciation ⎰   40 %

Physical Earnestness 10
Voice 10
Grouping 10
_____
General Effect   60 % -